Comments about Grace B... Beyond This Reality.

"We were so blessed to hear your story."
Rita Wilson, United Methodist Church, Madera, CA.

"Hurrah for publicizing your near-death experience. 'Ye shall know the truth and the truth shall set ye free."
Eve Lindquist

"I'm thrilled with your mission to share with the world."
Wanda Walters

"I learned a lot and gained comfort from your words."
Dr. Barbara McCallum, Your Peace of Mind Radio Show Host

"It was good to hear of your unfaltering courage in expressing your most truthful inner experience in the wake of so many skeptics. Always radiate your beautiful loving and knowing spirit."
Alix and Ronald Gavran, Authors, "Your Dream Relationship"

"I have gotten excellent feedback from your talk. It was a pleasure having you at our church."
Rev. Maxine Kaye

"What I found interesting about your story were the consequences of our words and actions on others in our life."
Jack Kollenda, Creative Writer, Huntington Beach, CA.

"I want to thank Grace for coming to the church. I was so moved by her tape that I had to find a way to have her speak to the congregation. The turn out for the service and workshop showed how moved the congregation was as well."
Kristin Wanden, Temecula, CA.

"Thank for being our 'Earth Angel' – You were wonderful."
Linda Moore, Compassionate Friends Bereavement Group

"The reassurance of pain relief takes away the fear of death and gives peace to the heart."
Anonymous, San Diego Hospice, CA.

"I was awed and believe every word of this. If everyone could/would accept these ideas, so much would be accomplished – to relieve the fear of death and dying which is why so many patients "hang on" even if the quality of their being would renew by death."
R. Crane, San Diego, CA.

Beyond This Reality

For Cora —
I hope you enjoy
my book
Sincerely,
Grace Bubulka Hatmaker

By
Grace Bubulka, R.N., M.S.N.

Bubulka, Grace
Beyond This Reality: A Personal Account of the Near Death Experience / by Grace Bubulka
ISBN 1-884995-03-9
1. Near-death experiences. I. Bubulka, Grace
II. Title

Printed in the United States of America

Word
Dancer
Press

Fresno, California

*To everything there is a season,
a time for every purpose under
heaven.*

Ecclesiastes 3:1
(New King James Version)

*God is light; in Him there is no
darkness at all.*

I John 1:5

TABLE OF CONTENTS

PREFACE

My near death experience (N.D.E.) occurred over ten years ago. I can precisely recall every specific detail of the event to this day. That always strikes me as very odd since I find it hard to remember exactly what I ate for dinner last evening. It took me almost ten years, to become comfortable sharing my experience with others. Shortly after my N.D.E., I had trouble processing the experience...I could not understand it nor could I explain how the experience actually occurred to me. At the time of the experience, I was in labor, had a fever of over 107 degrees Fahrenheit and was being given morphine for pain. Some may say the medication caused a "hallucination." Others may attribute this NDE to the high fever or lack of oxygen. But there really was no explanation for the incredible details of my experience and the personal impact it had on my life that was beyond reality. Words inadequately served me as I tried to verbally communicate my N.D.E. to other people who were important in my life, my family, fellow professionals and the clergy. As someone from a professional health care background, I actually tried to doubt the event was something that really happened to me. I tried to explain to myself that it was a result of my physical state and the medical care I was receiving at the time. But I could not deny that this set of events truly happened to me and subsequently changed my entire perspective on life and death.

I learned to see the polite doubt reflected in the eyes of those with whom I confided my experience. When I shared my N.D.E., often I felt others' confusion, cynicism and/or patronization.

In time, I learned to keep this incredible experience to myself, restrained by a fear of what others may think. I had enough pride, self-respect and common sense not to allow myself to be labeled as an eccentric.

Every night, I would remember the wonderment of it all. I savored those moments and knew that it would last forever in my memory.

What I did not know in that very isolated time of my life was just how common near death experiences really are. Although, as a nurse, I frequently cared for patients who were dying, I only had a superficial and skeptical notion about people who claimed to have had out of body experiences along with seeing a light, hearing music and greeting loved ones during illness or as death approached. These experiences made interesting tabloid headlines that helped pass the time whenever I was stuck in a long supermarket check-out line but they most certainly lacked any scientific validity.

I began to review the literature and to find out that the experience is quite common. This surprised me yet it was also very comforting. Later an unusual sequence of events that led me to personally meet and talk with leaders and other experiencers in the field. These people supported me and some carefully disclosed their N.D.E.'s to me. They often used the same words I did when describing their experience. They often sounded just like me.

With the love and support of others who finally listened and understood, I was inspired to write about my personal experience. It is important that others read about the experiences that have become wide-spread in this country and in other countries. It doesn't really matter that people "believe" this. It is important to respect the experience and challenge the scientists to scrutinize it. The irony of it all is that everyone will find out for themselves at the time of their own death!

All I can say is that my N.D.E. has completely changed my life. My life will never be the same. As a result of my near death experience, in time, I learned three major lessons. First, I learned not to ever fear death again. The seeming pain of death is fleeting in the broad perspective of eternity. Second, I learned to live my life here with integrity, being true to myself. Everything I do, say or think matters and is connected intricately and uniquely with the rest of the world. Third, I learned that there is eternal life beyond that which I now know. I no longer have to hope that there is something beyond death. I continued to exist as the real me after my body had finished it's work in the physical realm. My spiritual faith has become a knowing and certainty that the end of life is just the beginning of something else.

ACKNOWLEDGEMENTS

Many people have supported and encouraged me as I wrote this book. I am so very grateful to them all. Foremost is a special person in my life, my dear husband Stan Unruh, who kept asking me for more details about this near-death experience and what it meant to me. Finally, I told him in a joking manner, "You'll have to read the book!" Then I started writing about years of pent-up emotion, remarkably vivid detail and specific recall appeared on my rough drafts. As my drafts became more clearly understandable to others that I envisioned benefiting by it, my data analyst at work, Rick Padgett took the typed manuscript home. He spent many hours refining and polishing it with care. Dr. Joe Fawcett, our family chiropractor, took a special interest in the book and completed the detail of manuscript editing.

So many others played an essential role in the book you are reading. I was inspired by the insight and personal assistance of Dr. Pat Fenske, the President of the International Association for Near Death Studies, who invited me to her home office in Philadelphia and challenged me to do my best work. Dr. Justine Owens at the University of Virginia entered my name into a database of thousands of other "experiencers" and was also very encouraging. Naomi Cutler, a writer for Life magazine, wrote the article that was included in their 1992 issue.

I thank Mary Wilson who shared her poignant story with me and the many others who told me of their incredible experiences. They said how important it was that this information be communicated so that it could help those who were dying, the bereaved and professionals who have clients needing their respectful understanding. They wanted to share with clergy, psychologist and others keeping their stories to themselves for fear of ridicule.

I thank all those who listened to my story with care and love. They never had to believe, only hear...but many did believe.

THE ILLNESS

It was alternating between a grey snow and an icy rain all day that Saturday. I had just finished working a tense ten-hour shift at the hospital. As the hospital's nursing supervisor, it was my job to supervise four relatively new nursing managers who were in charge of their areas over the week-end. The day's events for me included coordinating the emergency staffing to cover the hospital's various units and departments, responding to codes on the nursing units and calling in staff for unplanned surgeries. It was a hectic but steady pace. As I walked across the parking lot on my way to my car, my mind was spinning with thoughts of the day behind me and the evening ahead. By the time I would get my car on the road, the sun would be down, and the streets a treacherous sheet of black ice so I quickened my pace.

At home, my two children, Karen age three and Billy age one, were in the care of the babysitter. My husband was already on shift at the local police station.

Suddenly, a searing pain crossed my abdomen, shaking my mind to attention. I was five months pregnant and never expected any medical difficulties. The other children were born without problems and my check-ups had been routine. I had a slight problem with a fast and irregular heartbeat but otherwise things were proceeding routinely with this pregnancy. So, I reasoned, this pain was gas or fatigue or something not to be overly concerned with. I brushed away this ominous sign from a toughness born of growing up in tough Philadelphia environment. I prided myself in my physical stamina and ability to handle almost any crisis.

The walkway to the employee parking lot was already icy and the pain made me feel somewhat light-headed. I placed one boot carefully ahead of the other on the slick ice that was forming underfoot as the sun set. Again, a pain ripped across my abdomen, I leaned to steady myself along the downhill slope that led to my car. I finally reached the car, opened the door and positioned myself carefully into the drivers' seat. I sat in my car with an odd sense of foreboding for about ten minutes.

The light-headedness subsided so I began to rationalize away my symptoms again. After all, I had been up before dawn, worked a long stressful day and there was no relief in sight until the children and I were in bed.

I looked at my watch, calculated another half-hour onto the babysitter's salary and decided to hurry home to my children. In the back of my mind, I knew things were not right. The sharp pains had dissipated but it almost felt like mild contractions had started. Again, I determined this to be gas pains and cautiously drove on. By the time I got home, I was fighting waves of nausea and getting chills. Maybe I had a cold. The babysitter gave me a report on the children and my husband indeed had gone into work at the police department much earlier. I fed Karen and Billy then dressed myself into comfortable night clothes trying to remain calm. The kids and I were in bed by 8:00 that evening.

I was exhausted physically and I lay in bed resting fitfully. I would doze off only to awaken shortly after my feelings of apprehension and bizarre dreams of going into labor. I felt incredibly alone and afraid. In the quiet, I listened to my babies sleeping and as the night dragged on I continued to get up to just check on them. Between the walks from my room to the children's rooms, I continued to review my day at work. All in all it went well. At work even the medical crises were orderly. There were written procedures and policies and generally people followed them. My personal life was not that orderly, however. As a new mother I learned quickly that small children lead very flexible lives. They always needed love and care but were somewhat unpredictable. My marriage was slowly falling apart it seemed. I kept trying to fix or ignore or otherwise deal with our ongoing difficulties. Finally, I just gave up assuming this was just the way marriage was and I needed to be a tougher individual.

About 1:00 A.M., I awoke with the shocking and accurate realization that I was very ill. I felt feverish. The shaking chills and the labor pains, that I thought were dreams, were actually occurring. I took my temperature. I took it again. The mercury was reading beyond the end of the thermometer, over 106 degrees Fahrenheit!

I called the police station and left word for my husband with the police dispatcher. I called my sister, Joan, in the event I would need a fast ride to the hospital or a babysitter. Then I called my obstetrician and he told me what I did not want to hear. I had to go back to the hospital immediately and he would meet me there.

A shower was my next plan...another knife-like pain across my abdomen and a gush of bloody fluid ran down legs. Did my water break? I stepped into the shower. The warm water flowing from the shower mixed with the tears sliding down my cheeks and the bloody fluid now pooling at my feet. I was standing in a shower of sadness. Chills and dizziness overtook me so I quickly got out of the shower. I pulled the clothes that I wore to work only hours before over my wet burning skin.

Deep inside of me I must have known this situation would be coming to a tragic ending. At the time though, I remember trying to be so tough and in control. That reaction, I am sure, was bred out of deep-rooted fear. I was alone. I was probably loosing my baby. I had two little ones to care for...and a disintegrating marriage. I could not afford the luxury of panic.

Zombie-like I called my sister who lived next door and told her I'd meet her at my front door so that she could take me to the hospital. She contacted family to watch the children. My sister, who is two years younger than I, can be very controlling. I needed that now. She supported me into her car. We drove carefully and silently through the night and back to the hospital. Joan looked straight ahead at the road, gritting her teeth with tension. I thought she must have been afraid to say much. Tears continued to fall from my eyes but I felt emotionally numb. The pain in my abdomen was becoming unbearable.

We pulled into a "reserved" parking spot near the Admissions entrance. Arm-in-arm we inched our way to the Admissions Office. In spite of the hour, the area was busy and we were instructed by the clerk to have a seat, fill in some forms and wait. I was so depressed at this point that I just sat in their chair on my blood-soaked bathroom towel.

My sister patted me on the arm then bounded into the supervisors' work area and took charge. Firmly, clearly and quite loudly she told them and everyone else in earshot that I was in labor and had to be taken to a bed immediately. I smiled inside with relief. I needed someone to take over...just for a bit, until I was well again.

I was seated in a wheelchair and whisked, too fast, into an awaiting emergency elevator. I remember watching other people watching me. I observed them out of my peripheral vision. They all noticed my pregnant abdomen and maternity blouse. Then they saw my head hung down with a puddle of tears forming on my lap. Then they quickly looked away.

The door to the Maternity/Gynecology floor on 5-West opened. Familiar faces greeted me in the surrealistic lighting of night shift in a hospital. Here were the nurses I just worked with a few hours ago. Several stayed on to work a double shift due to the weather conditions that effected staffing. I half expected a joke from one of them saying "hadn't you been here long enough today", but no one joked. I could see their concern that I was sick and that I was one of "them". Whenever a fellow nurse or doctor was ill, I was always a bit more concerned. They make terrible patients and heaven forbid something in their care goes wrong. These are people you work with and who are your friends.

They clustered about me and efficiently moved me into an area called the O.B.I.C.U....the Obstetrical Intensive Care Unit.

O.B.I.C.U.

Laying in my hospital bed I observed the activity at the nurses station once the staff completed the basic admissions procedure. I was in my hospital gown. Someone would be coming in to start the intravenous line soon. The nursing assistant left my room to get another thermometer since she did not think that the first temperature she took was accurate. Fevers nearing 107 just require re-checking since that is such a grossly abnormal reading.

The nurses station adjoined the large unit where I was admitted. I could see everything that the staff did and most of what they said by just lying there with my head turned to the left, facing them. Concentrating on their activity kept me from thinking, interpreting or accepting what was happening inside of my body. The nursing assistant seemed to be taking a long time but I was aware of the routine at the beginning of the night shift. The staff was busy and one by one the exhausted evening staff reported off on their patients and left the two nurses and the assistant to run 5 West. I listened to their shift report...of babies born and I.V.'s running and new mothers going home in the morning. Papers were shuffled, lights were dimmed and the night continued. A nurse came in before the assistant I expected to re-check my temperature. I did not know her but by now she knew I was one of the hospital staff. She chatted as she assembled her equipment preparing to start my I.V. I forced an "I hope you're good at that," lightly and she smiled. I realized when I spoke that my voice was shaking and my jaw was stiff. My head and my heart pounded. The contractions made my abdomen feel like a wooden board. As the nurse exposed my left arm, she whistled softly. The heat from my exposed arm rose to meet her. She looked at me with a shocked expression as she asked the other nurse to re-check my temperature. With a gentle touch, she positioned my arm for the IV placement.

She was taking great care but to me, she felt like she was twisting my arm in a vice. Every muscle in my body screamed with pain. I also began uncontrollable shaking. Thinking I was nervous the nurse encouraged me to calm down. The shaking was nothing I could control. Somehow, thanks to her obvious skill, she found a large vein and started the infusion of intravenous fluids. The bag hung on the I.V. pole at the left foot of my bed. As she taped the catheter securely to my arm, I stared at the bag swinging with the shaking of the bed caused by what were increasingly violent shaking chills. She popped the thermometer into my mouth then quickly retrieved it as I nearly bit the glass stem into pieces. She glanced at it assuming it had not yet registered, only to do a double-take. She put the thermometer close to the light at the head of my bed. She then showed it to me and asked, "Was it this high at home?" My vision was strangely blurry but I could see mercury stretch to the tip held firmly in her fingertips. With tears, I nodded yes.

She left quickly and headed back into the nurses' station. I heard stat overhead pages being announced to the extension I knew as the 5-West nurses station. The nurse snapped her assistant to attention and there appeared to be a great deal of activity at the desk.

The heat radiated from my body exaggerating every pain I felt, every sound I heard.

Another nurse entered. I did not know her but I will not ever forget her. Many of my patients have told me the same sort of thing. I can now understand what they mean. This was the nurse that helped me through my blackest night.

She appeared to be Filipino. I never knew her name. She spoke with a distinct accent but very softly. She carried a basin of water and had towels draped over her arm. She explained to me that until the doctors came, she knew what to do and would help me feel better. The words registered in my mind and I felt safe.

In silence, she pulled back my covers. As the air hit my burning body, the chills became like a seizure. My I.V. bag was swinging crazily and my every muscle felt as hard as my board-like abdomen.

She swiftly began sponging me with the cool water. The wash cloth felt like iced sandpaper but I knew she was doing the right thing.

The first nurse returned with a syringe. She told me the doctor ordered something for my pain and a suppository for my fever. I asked, "What am I being given for pain?" I was stunned to hear her reply, "Morphine". I told her, "Oh no, that will hurt the baby." The two nurses shot each other a knowing look of concern. She told me it was only two milligrams and the doctor was sure I needed this and that it was safe.

I remember thinking, "They never responded to what I said about the baby." Quickly, I avoided the thought that the baby might not survive anyway. I agreed, I needed something for pain. Two milligrams of morphine would probably not hurt the baby.

The sponging continued and my pain continued to increase. I continued to shake with fever. Thank goodness that one Filipino nurse stayed with me throughout the endless night. The interminable, doom-like night created a nightmare sensation. How long would this last? When will it be over? How will it be over?

My abdomen felt like it was splitting apart. There were no more contractions. I only felt a continuous overwhelming pain. Another dose of the ineffective and innocent morphine. "Where are the doctors?" I asked through gritted clattering teeth. They were "on their way."

I heard more stat pages. Behind me the assistant tried to quietly position the emergency code cart. I could tell that the cart was coming from the familiar clambering, squeaking, clanks it always made through the halls. Every week-end it seemed when I worked, we had to take the cart, which was complete with everything necessary to revive a patient to a bedside. Its appearance was not a good omen.

"Strange," I thought, "that the cart is here by my bed."

I was in a crisis and guessed I was losing my baby. Not for a moment did I think I could die.

I was sinking in a sea of pain. I began to pray...there was nothing else to do.

THE DOCTORS ARRIVE

I could hear their hurried footsteps before they arrived at my bedside. My obstetrician strode into my room with his resident following closely behind. "Well, how are you, Grace?" He always called me "little mother" when I was in for my check-ups. His use of my first name added an emotional chill to the physical chills that were rocking my bed. I tried to override the muscle stiffness and answer him. I couldn't get a clear word out in response. I lost my brief opportunity to reply to his greeting. The staff that were involved in caring for me got into a huddle. A cacophony of sounds could be heard emerging from the group. I picked out words and phrases... "107degrees... irregular... tachycardia... husband's been notified and is on his way in."

They broke out of the huddle like a team that knew their exact roles for the tasks at hand. I visually swept the group from left to right. Out of my left peripheral vision I could see that a wrapped surgical tray had been placed on top of the code cart. The nursing assistant removed the tray and placed it on the counter top. She carefully unwrapped the outer cloth cover using sterile technique. Sterile technique is a term used to describe the procedure of having no contact with the inner contents of the tray, so that the tray will not have any micro-organisms from the staff on the instruments. I knew the tray by it's size and shape. It was an emergency childbirth delivery tray. Within the wrappings were the surgical instruments and other supplies to proceed with a bedside emergency delivery. A dull thought sunk into my mind. My suspicions were right. I was in labor. My labor was abnormal. The baby might die. I was reluctantly letting pieces of reality enter my mind much to my overwhelming sadness.

The next person I saw to my left was one of the night nurses. She was peering intently at my intravenous line and recommending they start another one. The obstetrician ordered my I.V. "opened wide" so that the increased fluid would begin to counter effect the fever and my dropping blood pressure. Wires and electrode pads were passed by the assistant from the defibrillator/ monitor unit affixed to the code cart. The monitor assured me that they could continuously visualize the crazy tap-dancing my heart was doing in my chest. The defibrillator worried me. What if my heart could not continue to tolerate the increasing erratic heart rhythm? With the defibrillator, large electrode paddles would be placed on my chest and an electric charge would be sent through my heart. The charge would stop the erratic pattern and stop my heart, for a second or two. Then, if my heart stayed strong, it would resume its normal rhythm. If it did not restart, the medical staff would compress my chest manually. I did not want to continue to think of that.

The nurse attached the monitor wires to adhesive pads on my chest with the speed and sure-handedness of many years of experience. Sometimes, I thought, patients were very lucky to get this type of nurse in an emergency. Night shift often becomes the resting ground for many an expert clinical nurse that does not want to deal with the bureaucracy of the day shift when all the bosses are about.

The audible beeps of the monitor caught everyone's attention. The heart rhythm it signalled was not a good one. Fast irregular heart beats are very ineffective in transporting the vital oxygen-carrying blood to crucial organs such as the brain, the kidneys and the uterus. In irritation, my obstetrician turned off the audible reminder that nagged at the staff already under pressure. I gazed at the I.V. bag still swinging from my shaking. The pole clanked noisily. Someone reached up to the bottle and hung another bottle containing a mixture of three antibiotics that was connected to the main intravenous line. The combination of triple antibiotics was thought to be a good bet to counter the causative bacteria that was causing my raging fever. With the two bottles sharing the pole, the clanking noise was louder yet. The foot of my bed was the only space unoccupied by a person. This became the target spot for things being thrown about. Bloody drapes, used instruments, paper wraps were all tossed in this direction.

To the right of my feet was my little Filipino nurse. She worked quietly and efficiently by the sides of the two physicians. I looked at their faces and read their concern. Both physicians were tense, soaking in perspiration. I felt so bad for them. Usually it was me by their side, assisting them in an emergency. This was all backwards. Even in my pain, I wished I were not the source of this major fuss and it would all go away.

Repeated attempts were being made to detect my blood pressure in the left arm. Someone said, "It's 70 over 40". That is a sign that I was entering into a stage where there was an inadequate supply of blood reaching my vital organs. My heartbeat raced, stopped, skipped, reversed..."So strange", I thought. How much faster will it race? Would my heart stop? It was odd, that I never for a moment really thought I was in danger of death. I don't know if I was in such denial. I could not entertain this idea. People generally don't accept their own mortality.

From my left side the nurse said, "I can't get her blood pressure." My doctor snapped, "Palpate it!'" What this means is that if a blood pressure can be felt with the nurses' fingertips rather than heard with her stethoscope, there was still a chance I had some circulation to the "important" body parts. This is usually a sign that is ominous. If allowed to continue without correction or treatment of the cause, the patient could suffer a cardiac arrest.

I could feel her trying to detect a pressure. The resident was trying on my right arm. Finally the nurse said, "I can't get it." "S---!," the resident exclaimed.

A VIEW FROM THE CEILING

With that last word, everything changed. Finally, I found that the pain had a limit and that I had been released. I felt a sensation in my stomach like a person feels when dropping down from a roller coaster peak. This type of "butterflies-in-my-stomach" feeling was a fleeting ripple inside of me. I was then looking down from above the left foot area of my bed. The distance from my bed was as though I was against the ceiling corner. I could see the backs of the staff to the left of my bed and the faces of my doctors and the Filipino nurse. This was the perspective I had which describes my "position" in the room. It is important for me to note here, however, that I was not aware of having any body or form. I do not know how I saw or heard things with my body still laying below. It was as though I did not need my body's eyes to see nor ears to hear. I felt a sense of incredible compassionate sorrow for the medical staff. At this point, the commotion about my bed was frantic. The nurse on the left moved across the foot of the bed and to the right. In the process she collided into another member of the team. The staff pulled aside my gown and was grabbing at my intravenous line to increase the speed of the infusion. Things were being thrown about and obscenities were being shouted. I was greatly distressed now by their behavior. They were working against each other in their rush. I was extremely upset watching how the physicians physically pushed aside "my nurse" as she continued to try to wipe my legs with cold water to bring down my fever. It was almost as though I could feel a sense of shame or embarrassment from within her as she was treated that way. The words they used to each other upset me terribly. I strained to communicate with them. I tried to intervene and get between them to have them relax. I wanted to let them know there was no need for them to be so upset because I was really fine. I was more than fine. I felt wonderful! But they could not sense me. They were preparing to insert another intravenous line. They were pulling the code cart closer. They were shouting stat this, stat that and "S---!, s---!, s---!".

I was exasperated with them and with my futile attempt to connect with them. I had no strong feelings about my body lying on the bed. It was almost unfamiliar to me. I observed it with a detached, cerebral analysis noting its presence and pitiful condition within this chaotic scene of events. My body looked shiny and greyish-white in appearance. I had the sensation a person would if they looked at an animal killed on the highway — a need to glance at it, then a sense of mild revulsion.

I just remained there with a sense of hovering for what felt like forever. It was really only for seconds or minutes I suppose but time did not make any sense. Time did not seem to apply. It seemed irrelevant. It was un-attached to anything, the way I was. Time is only relevant when it is relative to the normal orderly sequential aspects of life. So I was there for a moment or for eternity. I cannot say but it felt like a very long time to me. In actual time, my blood pressure dropped for about seven minutes. I was aware that I was separate from my body yet somehow I continued to exist. The part of me that existed did not have anything to do with my body. I was completely comfortable and no longer in any pain. All of the distress I was in while lying in my hospital bed was gone. I felt like I was bobbing about in a warm bath. The fever, the contractions, the shaking chills were all behind me. I could not have been more comfortable, yet I could not convey this to the medical staff that was continuing to work on my body frantically. I desperately wanted to communicate with them. I could not fully relax and enjoy my new-found peace with the scene of the tension continuing on below me. I felt such inner turmoil. I finally moved toward the staff at the foot of my bed in an attempt to console them. This was the only moment that I knew I was different, separate from them. There was absolutely no way of getting their attention. It was futile and I was back against the ceiling.

THROUGH THE TUNNEL

The perspective I had of hovering against the ceiling looking down on the medical team ended. I was now facing up. This is hard to describe but my perspective of facing down and then up was like being flipped like a pancake. I was mercifully no longer connected to the frantic scene that was continuing around my body on the bed. I had no desire to be there or to continue to observe anything that remained behind me. I had no sorrow about departing. I felt no loss of my family or loved ones left behind. All that was behind me was cast off and no longer a part of what I was experiencing. I also began to move in the new space I had entered. While I was at the hospital room ceiling I was somewhat stationary. Now I was in motion. I was proceeding slowly in an upward and outward direction, slightly angled to the left. I was aware of being surrounded but I didn't know by what or by whom. At first it just seemed like a foggy greyness about me. As the speed of my upward and outward movement increased, the enclosing fog seemed to have a bright ending at the distance. The area to my sides and above and below me were like thickening, shiny, opalescent grey clouds. I remember at the early moments of moving ahead through this enclosure a brightness to my left where I could see through the cloud-like tunnel. Beyond the walls of my tunnel was a shimmering, glowing light. The light contained an infinite number of specks within it. The specks were moving about. Some specks were going fast, some slow. They were all going in different directions yet none ever touched or impacted with each other. The only comparison I can draw with what I saw was what a person can see if you look into a sunbeam. It looked like the dust particles that ride within a sunbeam. I remember smiling to myself (or at least having a happy, knowing feeling) that I was akin to these specks and they were journeying as I was between realities.

As I proceeded along, I was sensitive to the increased speed of my movement by a sensation of wind rushing by me. It was a combined feeling of a sound and movement of warm, comfortable air against me. With this progression I became increasingly relaxed. I felt as though I was anticipating something wonderful. At no point was I frightened. I had no remorse about leaving my body nor other people or loved ones behind.

I was also very aware of being helped through this transition. I was in company of an innumerable amount of others who were just like me. It was as though they were family . . . that I didn't know or I had forgotten. They knew all about me and were there to celebrate, comfort, ease and move me ahead. There was no sense of recognition but I knew they were there to help.

My tunnel structure thinned along the sides but the light ahead was beckoning me. I was intensely attracted to reaching the light. As the sides of the tunnel became clearer, the light ahead became brighter and closer as my speed increased.

The level of joyous anticipation I was feeling was indescribable. At this point I had no insight into what any of this was about. I did not think I was dead. I knew I felt like a spirit or a disembodied person. I knew that the real "I" continued to exist in the absence of my earthly body. I had a sense of heightened knowing, of peace and of assured expectancy.

ENTERING THE LIGHT

As I neared the warm, glowing radiance ahead of me, I felt pure ecstasy. I was like a metal filing being pulled harder and swifter the closer I got to the magnetic pull of the light. Even though I was being pulled, which describes a sense of something outside of me, I was desirous and eager to proceed. The warmth was heavenly. I felt like I was in a warm whirling liquid-like substance. I was in some substance thicker than air but thinner than water when my movement slowed to a gentle halt. I was in the beginning of the light. I was part of the light. The light was part of me...but the light was more. Somehow I knew there was more ahead but for now I could go no further because something was about to take place. I was still joyously content in the glowing warm whirlpool of light specks all about. The color was a gold. Not a metallic gold, not a crayon gold. It was like the gold of the sun if a person could really look at it. It was pure brightness but not painful to "view" or to be "in". I felt as if I had returned to something I knew before. It was as if I had come home. I had come home to the beginning of not just me but the beginning of all eternity. This is so hard to explain but it seems so important. The only thing this compares to in a way is the way it feels when it is a beautiful warm night and you look up into the clear starry sky. When you look at the stars, there is an awe of the glimpse at the beginning of infinite space. It was like that feeling as I savored my experience.

During this experience, time had no meaning. Time was an irrelevant notion. It felt like eternity. I felt like I was there an eternity. No remnants of the tunnel remained. There was no cloud or fog. The light was pure and all-good. I needed nothing, I wanted nothing. I was in communion with all the light around me. The specks, the others and I were all part of the light that existed forever. I felt I had an infinite sense of knowing, of understanding it all. I was completely at ease.

Then from within the light was a message. I received communication. I have no idea from where or how it came to me. There was no person there. No words were spoken. The thought was there for me to receive and accept. I was being reminded of my responsibility to my two children. I had the beginning of a notion to disagree...somehow. I did not want anything to change yet I could feel that a change had already begun. I no longer felt that something wonderful was just ahead for me. I was being "told" benevolently yet firmly of my duty. This message was the final word. . . it was all there was to communicate. I remember feeling a strain to hold onto my experience. I wanted to disagree while at the same time knowing it was point-less. I knew that from within the greatest part of all light was the complete wisdom that directed me. I felt like being a very small child whose loving parent in-sists and directs the tired child to bed. The directive was the only point. I had to go.

At this moment, I had one last type of communi-cation with this powerful part of the light. Suddenly, I saw it all. I saw me as I was as a baby, a child, a teen, an adult, all at once. At the same time, I saw everything I ever did, everything I ever thought, everything. I saw events and people in my life that I previously consid-ered important. Also, I saw many things that seemed-not-so important. I was aware of everything in my life all at once and I was aware of every response that oth-ers had to what occurred in my life. It was all there for me to understand... everything "good", "bad" or "indif-ferent".

For example, I remembered knowing deeply about a situation that I dealt with in first grade as a six-year-old child. I was in class and it was a few minutes before recess. Sister Celine had positioned three holy cards on the edge of her desk in the front of the room. The holy cards were to be awarded after recess in the spelling bee that our class would have. I was at the front desk and could see the holy cards well. The one in the middle depicted a gossamer guardian angel watch-ing over two small children crossing a bridge. I wanted that card so badly. As we filed out for recess, tempta-tion overtook me and I stole the holy card. I slipped it quickly into my uniform pocket. No one saw me. During recess, I felt sick with guilt. I snuck back into the classroom while the other first graders were playing at recess and placed the holy card back on Sister's desk.

In my near death experience I remembered everything about that situation. What was really impressive, though, is that I was aware how very wrong that action was. Although I had made amends I "knew" of Sister Celine's dismay at having the card taken. I "knew" that other children saw only two cards on the desk for the spelling bee, not three. What I really "knew" was that my action carried repercussions that effected many others.

This is the way my life was reviewed. I was deeply aware and had profound insight into everything in my life and all of my dealings with others from my birth on to the moment of my near death experience. All those in the light were witness to this review of my entire life. I was enveloped in a loving feeling and given insight into areas of my weaknesses. I suddenly realized aspects of my life that were not compatible with eternity in the light. I also knew now how to correct this. I was charged with the accountability of the remainder of my life.

I knew that more was ahead in the light that continued forever but I could not go there now. Seeing my life left me with the impression that my life mattered and was somehow significant as to how far I could go into the light. My work was not yet finished and my work was to begin inside me and within my family.

I was able to concede to my impending return now that I fully understood the message.

Then I was given a "gift" to ease my return...or at least that is how I interpreted this at the time. As the brightness began to dull, the image of my two children were merged into my spirit. As I held their love in me, I returned to my body in the hospital bed.

THE RETURN FROM BEYOND

It felt like a truck hitting a wall at full speed. I re-entered my body. I went from a sense of departing that loving blissful light to the most horrible sensation I can ever describe. My body was racked with pain. Every muscle, every cell of me hurt. Medically, my unborn son and the attached placenta had separated and torn away from the lining of the womb. With one ghastly, abnormal contraction and a gush of bright red blood, my son was born. I sat half-way up from the bed and shouted an echoing "no" as I saw him unfold from the curled up position he had when he was inside of me. He seemed to part his arms slowly and drop back his head. He was limp and greyish with his mouth and eyes partially opened. He was dead. A nurse put his body in a cold hard metal emesis basin. That made me feel so sad. I know that made no sense but if only they'd lay him on a blanket or a soft towel. The staff though were so excited that I "was back". They shouted to me "you're back". They were so happy, so proud of themselves. They had successfully resuscitated me. My challenge to them was not over since the placental delivery was imminent, but I was more medically stable. All noise and light seemed exaggerated to me. It sounded as though they were screaming. I fell back against the pillows as the placenta was delivered with the next contraction and the doctors controlled my bleeding. One of the nurses bent close to me at my right ear. She said, "Grace, you're going to be okay now. You had us worried," with sincere cheerfulness. I closed my eyes and turned my head away from her with anger. It's funny that I often recalled my patients reacting the same way. They didn't seem happy. Sometimes they cried. Sometimes they seemed angry. They never seemed grateful to us for all the hard work of reviving them. I listened to them change the combination of antibiotics that were going into my I.V. to deal with the infection. I watched through partially closed eyes as the head nurse of the obstetrical I.C.U. quietly baptized my son's shiny, redish-grey body as he lay curled there in that metal emesis basin on the counter next to the sink. I let the medical staff think that I had fallen asleep for I did not want to communicate with them. I hated them. I hated the world. I hated the pain and my innocent son's death. I hated my departure from the light to this crass world of sorrow. It all looked crude and awful to me. I knew they wouldn't understand.

In minutes, the fever that was raging in my body began to dissipate. My uterus firmed up as the bleeding slowed. My vital signs began to stabilize and my heart beat was more regular. The physicians in the room were busy validating and approving of their recent decision to change antibiotics. They also academically hypothesized the idea that my son was contributory, if not the source, of the state of sepsis that I had been in. My skin that had been ice cold and pouring perspiration, then on fire with fever was starting to feel like my normal skin. My hair was soaked and I was laying in a pool of blood, sweat, amniotic fluid and now tears. My tears streamed out of my tightly closed eyes hoping that no one would see. No one did, thank goodness . . . or no one acted like they did.

The physicians who were with me throughout the ordeal almost all of the night were reviewing my orders and treatment plan but mostly they just needed to go on to their other patients or to sleep. The nurses really had a chore. The room was a trash heap of soiled linens, surgical wraps, medical instruments, emergency equipment, charts, medications...and my son's body. I continued to play possum as they went about their duties. Either they thought I was sleeping or they were allowing me to shut out the world. They were remarking among themselves about the mess and relieved the emergency had ended successfully. The emesis basin containing my son's body was placed on top of the emergency cart with the other discarded stuff and wheeled out of the room. I longed to touch him but I was afraid that was not appropriate. I was afraid they would think it was abnormal or a gross thing to do. All I really wanted to do was touch his little hand and stroke his head. Since no one offered, I did not ask. The nurse who then tried to change my sheets and clean me up attempted to talk with me kindly. I shot a look of anger in her direction and refused to communicate. She handed me some tissues for my tears and continued the major clean up job at hand. I did not want to be here. I did not want to be any part to this terrible scene.

I fell asleep. For hours my body just shut off and I slept a dreamless sleep of exhaustion. When I awoke and looked to my side, my roommate in the next bed was staring at me with her eyes bugging out. She said, "Honey, I ain't never heard anyone scream like that in my entire life. Are you okay?" I asked her if I screamed and then I remembered the birth of my child. I remember shouting "no" but did I scream? Then I remembered the pain and my horror of seeing my perfectly formed dead child. Yes, I must have screamed.

My roommate was calling for the nurse to help me. I was sobbing in sorrow at my loss. The nurses came in and checked my blood pressure. They told me they would be transferring me soon to a private room. From my experience as the hospital supervisor, I knew about that room. That was the room for grief stricken mothers. That room was where mothers recovered from stillbirth deliveries. It was the room used for mothers who were putting their babies up for adoption. How I hated that room as a Nursing Supervisor. I never knew what to say. The patients in that room were so unpredictable. Every other mother on the floor was cooing and holding their babies. These mothers were overcome by inconsolable grief and personal anguish.

Reality was now taking hold and I could not allow myself to be hysterical. I decided to be stoic . . . something I had always been rather good at. I was wheeled into my room. The room had a huge picture window with a breathtaking view of suburban Philadelphia. I was too weak to sit up yet so I laid in bed looking into the stark blue March sky through the window.

Then I remembered. My tunnel, the light, my duty, the love. As I looked out into the sky, I realized my son was not gone. He still existed. His body was finished but he was still living on. A touch of comfort began to effect my emotional pain. That light was a gift, an assurance of life beyond death.

I looked around with embarrassment. I was fearful of anyone knowing the thoughts I was having. I had heard about "post-partum psychosis." My thoughts sounded bizarre, even crazy to me.

I relaxed finally because inside of me I really knew what I experienced was true. I really knew that my son's soul went home to live on with the wondrous light specks in the warm everlasting bliss. Through the tears I felt a soft smile briefly light my face. I imagined my son was fine and somehow so would I be fine.

I comforted myself with this but could not share my experience. I began to tell a nurse and I saw the alarm and disbelief in her face. She charted something in my medical record. Oh, no. I began to tell my husband and I saw his patronizing, cynical denial of its truth. He cautioned me that if I keep talking like that they'd probably lock me up.

I decided I would tell no one. I did not want this apparently delusional thinking documented on my medical record. I did not believe anyone would believe me. My experience was so hard to put into words. I also was weak and still sick from my physical ordeal and labor. I needed someone to just hear what I experienced without judgement. I needed the emotional support to relate the details of everything I had been through. I knew the experience had meaning . . . that it had a very important message. Every time I tried to figure out the obscure nature of its meaning by sharing it with others, I was blocked. I was met with patronization, doubt, gentle ridicule. It was as though I had a precious delicate and fragile gift. Each time I handed it to someone they dashed it to the ground causing me great emotional pain. Perhaps, I thought, the message is only for me. For now it is helping me cope with the loss of my son. Maybe in time I'll understand the rest of it all . . . my separation from my body, being joined by others, the awe-inspiring indescribable Light I could not fully reach and my life review.

I went back to sleep.

THE FOLLOWING DAYS

Flower arrangements arrived. Many greeting cards were delivered to my room in the hospital. They seemed all the same to me. They carried the awkwardness of "What do I say?" Flowers saddened me since they were cut from their life to make the pretty arrangements. Cards seemed so strange..."get well soon", "thinking of you", "in sympathy".

The medical staff who were my friends and co-workers became very professional and somewhat perfunctory in my care. I couldn't blame them. Any time one of them would offer a kind word or make eye contact with me, I would practically bite their head off or start crying again.

A doctor came in and had me sign permission for my son's autopsy. He asked me if I wanted to have either a service or funeral/burial. He also offered to "take care of it". With grief, I told him to take care of "him" and that I could not emotionally tolerate a funeral. He explained vaguely that a local burial site would be used after the autopsy. I still wanted to hold my baby and I wanted to touch him. But I was ashamed to ask. Too much time had gone by. He was probably in that cold morgue now.

It all seemed so grotesque. I told the doctor to leave. I stood in the shower crying for the next half an hour as milk ran from my swollen breasts for a child who was gone from me.

I composed myself and crawled back to bed. I could hear a great deal of excited commotion and talking outside of my room. One of the nurses came in to tell me that President Reagan was shot. I didn't care. I had no interest whatsoever in world affairs or anything else. I needed to get strong enough to get out of the hospital.

An unfortunate Catholic priest came into my room next. He was an overweight man in his late fifties. He was bent over a pack of index cards in his hands. He looked at the number on my door and began to bestow a Catholic blessing. Since I was no longer a practicing Catholic, I said, "Father, what do you want?" He looked down at his cards and then up at me. He said, "Congratulations, Mrs. Ryan, I see we had a beautiful healthy little girl!"

Rage for everything that had happened to me boiled to the surface. Immodestly, I bounded out of my bed toward the shocked priest. I raised my hand and pointed my finger in his face and said, "he's a boy, he's dead and now get out!"

The poor priest nearly dropped all of his cards, mumbled a "bless you" and escaped my room at great speed.

I called the nurse, told her what happened and asked her to get the doctor to discharge me in the morning. At this point I did not trust my anger nor my recollection of the tunnel and the light...I wanted out!

My husband came to visit and briefly sat alongside my hospital bed. "I *have* to tell you about this really strange experience," I insisted. As I told him excerpts from my experience he looked at me with doubt and skepticism. I paused at his reaction. Finally, he feebly joked, "Like I said before, keep talking like that and they'll lock you up in the psych unit."

As I would try to convey my thoughts to the medical staff I saw their confusion and concern.

I stopped trying. I just wanted to get out of that hospital.

EMBERS REKINDLED

The nurses who stood by me through this ordeal continued to accept my emotions and assist in my recovery. They helped me pack up belongings. They needed a separate cart for all of the beautiful flowers and gifts that had been sent to me when words failed their senders. The nurse who tried so hard to bring down my fever carefully eased me into the wheelchair. I caught a glimpse of myself as I was wheeled by a mirror. I was ghastly white with dark circles ringing my puffy red-rimmed eyes. My body was bent over in a depressed exhaustion. My thin blonde hair hung shapelessly from my head. A group of my friends were standing by the nurses station as my chair was paused courteously before passing them. I could only look at the hems of their uniforms. I was sure if I looked up I would begin to cry and they would decide I needed to stay or see the doctor again.

I had just finished a brief meeting with my doctor and I did not want to go through another discussion with him. He held many slips of paper as he sat beside me on my bed. The required autopsy had been completed on my son's body. He told me that there was nothing abnormal about him but the baby and surrounding fluid tested positive for a bacterial/viral infection. He explained this the best he could. Although my baby was normal, the infection I got was the cause of his death and almost took an ultimate toll on me. He told me I had been in septic shock and had an abruptio placenta which meant a premature separation of the placenta from the womb causing severe bleeding. He assured me that the baby could not have survived and the morphine that I was given did not hurt him. He said if they had tried to resuscitate the baby after he was delivered and if he had lived he would not have been normal. My doctor then handed me some papers. I also received prescriptions for hormones and an appointment slip for a follow-up visit. After all the paper had been passed, he finally looked at me and said "I'm sorry". The tears continued to leak from my eyes as I nodded my acceptance of this and he left the room. I could feel his sense of defeat.

I had to be wheeled past a group of my co-workers at the nurses station soon. I knew they felt sorry for me and for themselves. I wished this had not happened to me or to them.

I was assisted into the car and drove with silent tears along side my stone-faced husband. I kept trying to tell him again about leaving my body. He looked at me with a shocked looked and we said no more for the rest of the ride through the stark, dirty Philadelphia streets toward home.

My experience coming home was even more uncomfortable than the situation at the hospital. My sister had been caring for the children but they were quickly shushed and kindly removed away from me. My husband offered to make me some tea. I refused. I sat in the living room on the corner of the sofa with a box of tissues and a bag for the used ones. The window shades were pulled down and the room was grey. The hospital flowers looked as beaten down and as wilted as I felt. The doorbell rang and I heard my parents at the doorstep. They held what seemed to be a long conversation with my husband at the door then they tip-toed into the living room. A few awkward words were exchanged...but really, what could be said. I told them I had the most unusual experience of being separated from my body. Furtive glances were passed around the room. I was learning quickly that my experience was a taboo topic of discussion. This situation would repeat itself with others consistently, again and again. I was looked at with either pity, shocked disbelief and/or patrontization.

The door-bell continued to ring off and on for days. Most people would come to the door to offer their condolences but most did not come in. They often whispered politely at the door "is she okay". I felt like screaming at them that I had not gone deaf and I would be okay. They generally said I needed my rest and they did not want to disturb me. This was very disheartening and terribly depressing. The people I cared for could not override their fears. They projected onto me a level of fatigue that prevented their visitation. I just needed a compassionate listening ear. The church pastor came and did provide that. He listened briefly, professionally and humanely. Among most, however, the reaction was withdrawal until "Grace pulls herself out of this."

Every day I would sit in the darkened living room and replay it all over in my mind...the pain, the birth, the tunnel, the light understanding my life and my directive to do something. I couldn't "believe it" myself, so how could others. Yet I could not deny the experience happened. I thought possibly the medications caused the "dream". Perhaps the decreased blood supply precipitated a "hallucination". Maybe the fever affected part of my brain. That was all partially plausible but how do any of those things describe the detailed order of events in my experience? They were so deeply meaningful to me. This was not just an abstract disjointed dream. I had never experienced, thought or imagined anything of such magnanimous truth. At bedtime every night, as I finally relaxed to sleep I recalled the light and what I needed to do. I was told . . . no, actually, commanded to lead my life in truth and light. Yet, I lay there not knowing where to start or how to shake my depressed sorrow.

After about two weeks the door-bell rang less frequently. Life was going on about me and I was beginning to perform the routine activities of daily living and child-rearing in a zombie-like fashion. I was going through the motions and people about me were relieved. As I began to show some return to the old Grace, people began to respond to me accordingly. Small talk filled the small conversations and I started to plan ahead for my return to work and to school. As long as I could put on a good act, I was acceptable...WHAM! It hit me. What I was told in the light could no longer be avoided. I could no longer put on a good act for others. I was commanded to live a good true life to the best of my human ability. I was neither told to please others, to obey the rules and conform nor to stifle myself. For the first time in a long time I smiled as a warm glow filled my heart. Now I knew that this is really where the hard work begins. Yet this is good work. This is where I started. I started with this moment in my life and lived every precious moment measured against the light. Every precious moment, every current one and those to come in my life would be reviewed. I was being given another chance. Slowly, cautiously I began to put my life into place. My every thought and action from then on had to be held up to the light. Things I had avoided for years could no longer be avoided. There are no corners in which to hide when you live a life in the light. I had never seen what a significant role conflict-avoidance had played in my life. Each day I tried with absolute resolve to stay in the light.

The light was always with me through this time of my life. When I sat for two weeks in my darkened living room among the faceless whispers of well meaning visitors. The light was an ember in the darkness of my mourning soul. Now the light was my shield, my companion, my hope and a guiding force.

I no longer needed to try to relate my experience to others. It hurt that they wouldn't listen. Their withdrawal from me was painful but now I knew I'd be okay. The light had put me on a path that would stretch across the rest of my years.

It was almost as though my life leading up to that experience was a life of darkness. It was like trying to walk down a rocky path in the forest at night. Suddenly, I was provided with a great Light. This illumination made my path easy to see. It didn't take away any of the rocks or obstacles in my way . . . but it did make my way clear to see and to proceed.

BACK INTO THE LIGHT

The years that followed my near death experience were the years that contained the most significant and meaningful changes in my life. I was set back on the right track by my experience but by no stretch of the imagination was my life easy or straightforward after that. I knew the standard by which to measure everything I did, said, saw, felt and thought. The measurement was that total, pure, perfect, wise Light.

For starters, I began to feel differently about myself. I felt an inner strength I had never previously felt. Everything in life was now brought into perspective. I knew I had within my power all I ever needed to live my life correctly. I had this all along but now I knew this. I felt fortunate, blessed for having had my experience. My memory of my near death experience was my secret friend and my constant companion. I was reflective now about everything I experienced. I looked at things with a clearer insight and understanding, acknowledged inconsistencies in my life that I could no longer tolerate. Although I lacked the experience and the practice to proceed on this new wisdom, at least I knew where I needed to go as I re-evaluated my life.

My perspective of the world changed, if this makes any sense. I saw the world as it was intimately connected with everything within it and beyond it for all eternity. I could see how I was part of the whole and everything was a part of me. This connectedness can be explained on a more mundane level when you consider a man getting out of bed grouchy in the morning. He speaks gruffly to his children. His children go to school with the burden of his anger on their minds. They effect several teachers who are having difficulty teaching them. The teachers impart their frustration on thirty students each who all go home after a bad day and argue with their siblings who in turn bother the neighbors who speak to others on the phone that evening who then upset others and so it goes. All because of one grouchy man. Suppose there are several of these grouches on any given day! Suppose they are not just grouches but rather thieves or rapists. You see it is all connected. Every action, every deed, every word has the potential to effect the universe. Can you imagine the catastrophic effect one person could have? I have heard this idea since, very well explained by my pastor. He said it is like the story of a little boy who is standing beside a completely still lake. He takes a pebble and tosses it into the lake. He feels very proud watching the ripples it makes. That one small stone makes ripples that soon cross over the entire lake and the boy is very impressed with the effect caused by his action. What the little boy does not see, however, is the pebble also makes waves in the water below the surface where we cannot even see. We have no idea how far or how deep even our tiniest actions go. We cannot see the impact we have on others or on our surroundings even at very far distances. It is imaginable that every one of our actions, our thoughts, our attitudes whether they be positive or negative has the potential to effect the entire world. Like that pebble in the lake, our relatively small personal pebbles create ripples and undercurrents touching upon all of life. That is a humbling thought. It all starts within each of us keeping true to our own personal lights. I felt so fortunate for having gotten so close to the light and what felt like "peeking-in" on eternity. I know now what was ahead of me. For now, though, I had a responsibility to my loved ones and to those that I did not love to be true to myself and to share myself truthfully with them. I knew I had to face major relationship issues that I had been ducking away from for years. I slowly and painfully dealt with my disintegrated marriage and ended it in divorce years later. This was a significant emotional toll but one in which I had to finally face and resolve the on-going problems that would never change. Why did a decision finally come after such a long time. Well the experience shed clarity on my situation. I was still very much the same person I was before with a brand new perspective. I continued to try, to confront and to challenge only to finally accept my marriage was over and really had been for years.

My relationship with my family and friends changed too. I had been role-playing for the most part of my life. Afraid to speak up or to assert myself or express independent thought, I led most of my life in a good-girl mode. I was rarely other than well-behaved and pleasant. This was a mask though. Inside of me was an unexpressed anger at the inability to have myself heard. As I continued to stay in this role those around me continued to reinforce it. It was comfortable for them as well that I not "make waves". I was shielded from much of reality by friends and family for they usually perceived me as somewhat weak and frail. Often feeling isolated and depressed I was usually my only companion. Alone, I kept company with books and study. When my marriage pressure became overwhelming I drank wine. When I could not deal with the patronization, I slept for hours and hours. As you can see I lived in a vicious cycle of fear, shame and avoidance. Now things were different and I began to be more interactive and clear about myself. Needless to say, I shook up the old status quo. Things were quite out of balance for awhile. The only way most of my family and friends could relate to this difference, was to attribute it to the stress of losing my baby. My story of the light made no sense to anyone other than me. I was thought to have a significant emotional response to my ordeal.

I had been raised a Roman Catholic and until my teen years considered myself to be "a good Catholic." As a little girl I followed the rules of the Church and was dutifully obedient to the nuns and priests. At one time I wanted to be a nun, a sister of the Immaculate Heart of Mary. I was devout and felt I could be like the nuns who taught me in school or worked in the hospital. By the time I was in high school I began to challenge the Church's rules. Raising these types of questions were inappropriate. My family and the religion just admonished me to believe and pray. By my college days, I had given up on Catholicism and became engaged to a Protestant boy I later married. We rarely went to church but when the children were born, going to church seemed important for us to do again. It was an empty, hollow experience. Even though I was back in church I was very superficial in my spiritual life.

The Sunday after my hospital discharge was different.

I remember my first Sunday going to church after my near death experience. I could now understand phrases that I had only recited like a parrot since I was a child. For example, when the Apostle's Creed was being recited by the congregation a set of words hit me with a clarity of amazing proportion...the communion of saints!! I could not believe I was hearing these words! I must have said the "communion of saints" within the creed literally hundreds, if not thousands of times, since I was a child. Now I knew what that meant. It meant that union of infinite specks of eternal light that I had communed with as I entered the warm wonderful glow. That's who and what was there. I was surrounded and supported by others such as I. We were all souls. We were that pure spiritual part of us without our earthly bodies. I suppose if they remained in the light they were the communion of saints. Since I returned, I felt short of their state of brilliance but now the words began to make sense.

I quickly sat down (in spite of the fact that everyone else was still standing). I started flipping through the Bible that I had pulled out from the rack in front of me...incredible!!! I could spot reference after reference to the Light, the Word, the Source. I grabbed a hymnal...Nearer My God To Thee. Everything I noticed had some connection. Could it be that the wisdom in the Book or the hymnals were attempts to convey others' experiences with the light? Could it be forever man has been trying to make contact with his creator, the One who made all and loves us so beautifully? I was struck, here too, with aspects of religious teaching that were truly made by man. Things of a legalistic value or of ritual or of performance were not true. These things were man's attempt to connect and harness what is good and to ward off evil...a good try, I thought, for humans.

I began to treat my body differently as well. I had taken my body for granted. I did not care for it and tend to it as I should have. Again, I had insight into the words that the body is the "temple of the Holy Spirit". My spirit, the one that hovered on the ceiling, traveled through the tunnel and merged into the beginning of the gold was in a shelter that I needed to care for. Everything I put into my mouth was now to be re-assessed. Foods for strength and balance and growth were important. Alcohol was poison. Excess was sinful. Denial was equally sinful. Inhaling second-hand smoke tarnished my body and effected every cell of my human form. I started eating with care. I took time and appropriate attention to grooming. I exercised and oxygenated my body. Slowly, over months, my pale, sunken form regained a health it nearly never had.

I assessed things and possessions and was shocked at how transparent my previous priorities were. I only need a few "things" and I needed to take good care of them.

Slowly, my body, my mind, my surroundings, my family and my "act" was cleaned up. But I realized all that I was experiencing was a process for I was not in the light now but in the world with a bit of the light within me. What that meant is every day I would deal with people and issues that were rooted in worldly values and had worldly priorities. Yet, the light within me helped keep it all in perspective for me.

It was time to evaluate the reality of my marriage. For so many years I had avoided the issues that slowly and insidiously were eroding our relationship. Now I needed to confront it.

I did not like what I saw. Over the years the relationship had begun to die. Dealing with problems in a straight-foreword manner was going to be difficult. The outlook looked bleak but I felt stronger and able to deal with the situations as they unfolded... and finally several years later, my divorce.

MY RELIGIOUS BELIEFS

I have heard people assume that the person who reports a near death experience is a highly religious, bible touting believer. The near death experience occurs in people who are devout Catholics, devout Buddhists and devout atheists as well. The experience is one that is not limited to a particular denomination that has been established by man. It does, however, contain what most consider to be an impressive spiritual component that is easily interpreted along the lines and language of a religious experience.

As I said, I grew up as a Catholic. I was baptized as an infant, received my first Holy Communion in second grade, was Confirmed in third grade, had the "calling" in eighth grade and had a special devotion to the Blessed Virgin Mary throughout high school. Those reading this who were raised Catholic will know the significance of the stages that I just mentioned. These were common milestones that marked the spiritual growth of a young person growing up in the Catholic faith. Throughout this period, though, I always had a bit of an ongoing battle within me. Most of the Catholic churches were mysterious. I could not understand the Trinity, the combined Father, Son and Holy Ghost in one. What did communion of saints mean? How was a virgin birth possible? The Mass and devotions were recited in Latin. The rituals of the holy mass defied explanation. With the ringing of a bell, water was miraculously changed to wine. How was this to be believed? Yet in spite of my questions, I "believed"...or for many years I tried to believe. In my twenties, I rejected Catholicism. I rebelled against that which I could no longer accept nor understand. As I rejected the faith of my youth, I was left with a vacuum...a need to be filled. For as much as I disclaimed the church's teachings, I very much remained true to my own image of a personal loving God though. I no longer fit in the slot of a good Catholic. I ascribed to the less legalistic Protestant faith and considered myself to be a good Christian. At the same time I really did not know what that really meant. For a decade or so I fished around in my religion still needing a solid spirituality to sink my soul into. I rebelled at legalism and felt scornful towards religions that seemed too watered down.

My near death experience dramatically changed my luke-warm commitment to the God who made me and all that is in the universe and beyond. My near death experience put me in close contact with the power, the source of it all. I realize that the religions of this life are man's earnest attempt to connect with God. They all have the humanness and failings of man and I can now accept this. I can now connect the words of the prophets and the words in my hymnal and the words of the Bible. My N.D.E. taught me about universal love and forgiveness. I learned about how everything is connected and that everything matters. It taught me to value what is important in my life. It taught me to live my life. Slowly, day by day, actually second by second I had to apply this insight to the way I was conducting myself. I knew once again I would be facing an evaluation of my life. This time I needed to live what remained of my years in accordance with the light.

Eleven months after my near-death experience, I gave birth to my youngest daughter. After her birth, I became a true Christian.

I remember many years ago when I was working in a nursing home being cornered by three evangelistic church people. They wanted to know if I had been "saved." I had never learned what was meant by this term but to avoid their zeal I told them yes. Not to be put off they pressed on to ask if I had a personal relationship with the Lord. Well that did it! I called security and got those nuts out of my nursing home. My patients were confused enough. I didn't want these Christians stirring things up with their probing questions.

Now I know what that personal relationship is all about. It is as though, as small and insignificant as I am in the sense of eternity, my Maker cares for me individually. He loves me as he loves all, with complete understanding and only one request . . . to follow Him.

Yes, I became "reborn." I redirected my life and began to tackle real life issues. My life was far from simple from that point on. My near-death experience made me aware that I needed to deal with life. I could no longer ignore problems... they had to be addressed with integrity and with love. So much of my life had been spent in the avoidance of conflict and subsequently, as a result a lack of growth. The parables of Jesus, the stories from the Bible came alive as I began to apply them to my life. This life was not meant to be problem free. The reason for the challenges in my life was to grow into a stronger and better person so at the end of my life I could see it all again with peace and satisfaction for all eternity and perhaps next time go further into that glorious Light. As hard as it was, though, I felt supported and guided by the light. This experience, by the way, did not make me perfect. It just made me see and know. To this very day, I now know when I do wrong and I am compelled to correct myself. I don't deny problems...I can't for very long now. I say what I think or feel. I relate to others with more sensitivity but mostly with truth.

In the light I found my personal true spirituality that enabled me to fully commit to my Savior who would support me throughout my life.

COMMONLY ASKED QUESTIONS

WHY DID YOU WAIT SO LONG TO PUBLICLY SHARE YOUR STORY?

My near death experience occurred over ten years ago. I only began to share the complete details of the experience to a select group of trusted friends last year. This is not an unusual response for the near death experiencers. Experiencers report three typical responses which thwart their attempts to communicate their experiences. First, a message they usually receive is a strong non-verbal response denoting shock, disbelief, concern or fear. People listening to the story may feel the experiencer is hallucinating, crazy, or flat out lying. This reaction tends to close down communications for the experiencer. He does not want to be received this way. He sincerely wants to describe what really happened to him. Second, the experiencer sometimes is gently but straight-forwardly told that he is better off just "getting over" this or should spend time "resting". This type of response is very patronizing. It communicates that the person who had the N.D.E. is off balance in his thinking. This is very difficult for the experiencer as well because he struggles to find words for things, feelings and perceptions that defy clear definition. Third, the experiencer may meet out-right hostility and a challenge to him personally. This is also a very upsetting response since there is no reason for such anger. Once again the person who has had a N.D.E. is trying merely to communicate his experience. There is no need to convince others or to prove anything.

As I began to share my story, I found others would confide in me since, in their minds, I understood.

When I attended a national conference of the International Association of Near-Death Studies, I met hundreds of people who had experiences that they had kept to themselves for many years. Older people explained that in the "old days" you really would "get locked up for talking out of your head." Professionals and business persons did not want to bring discredit to themselves. Some simply did not want the curious attention it caused. Now, they were all most willing to share . . . however, somewhat selectively.

WHAT IS YOUR MOTIVATION TO TELL YOUR N.D.E. STORY?

People are curious about the person who reports a near death experience. Many are highly suspicious that the experience is an attempt to achieve a secondary gain from this experience. They may feel motives lie in notoriety or an increased status. The near death experiencer will attest that any attention that is brought to him about his experience is often negative, doubtful or neutral. The experiencer may achieve some notoriety for having reported this odd event after a life threatening illness or injury but since the experience challenges logic, the attention is not lasting nor is it significant.

Money as a motivator is also fruitless. Since there is a mixture of receptivity on the subject and is nearly impossible to describe clearly, there is little to be gained monetarily from the near death experience.

Stories of the near-death experiences told by young children are impressive to the skeptics. Children can be very clear and outspoken about their near-death experience and use child-like expressions or drawings to show just what it was like for them. Their motivation is purely to tell their story.

I personally found three strong and compelling reasons to re-tell my near death experience. First, I needed to have my experience heard by others as a means of processing this critical event into my life. The telling of my near death experience to those who listened and accepted without judgement provided an incredible amount of emotional relief for me. I felt unburdened. Second, I felt a personal responsibility to tell about my near death experience. If the N.D.E. is estimated to have been experienced by eight million people and it continues to be viewed with skepticism then it is incumbent for the experiencers to share their stories with the lay and scientific communities. Only when this event can be looked at openly and without bias and taboos, can some very basic empiric research questions be answered. Third, if the telling of this story helps other experiencers, families who have lost loved ones or those facing terminal illness, then it is worth the effort.

For example, one day when my experience was covered by our local newspaper, my office got a call from parents of a young girl who had died weeks before at the hospital where I worked. Since I was in charge of the Trauma Department of the hospital and since this child died of cancer, I was very concerned. Had I caused this bereaved family additional sorrow? Did telling my story hurt them? They were quite adamant that they did not want to talk to me on the phone. They wanted to schedule a meeting time and drive two hours from their home to talk with me. We set the appointment for the next day after work. I was so nervous. Finally, it was time to meet them. This mother and father stood for a moment at my office doorway. I didn't know what to say or do. I asked simply, "What?" Then both of them leaned forward and hugged me in a fervent embrace. I said "I don't understand." They asked to sit down and by then all three of us had tears in our eyes. They told me all about their beautiful little girl. The father took her photo out of his wallet with trembling hands. She was so precious and she reminded me of my youngest daughter. They told me how sick she was with cancer and what her final days in the hospital were like. As their daughter began to lapse in and out of consciousness she would tell her parents not to be sad. She told them that a boy who she knew that died at the hospital was waiting to help her. She told them she would be really happy. Her parents told me what a relief that was to them to know somehow their daughter would be at peace. Then they waited. They said, "Tell your story." It helps people like us. It helps others understand us when we tell them about our little girl. With another set of tearful hugs they quietly left.

That's my motivation for telling my story.

DO YOU REALLY BELIEVE THAT?

I was flying to the east coast recently on a business trip and was engrossed in a book about near death experiences in children titled "Closer to the Light" written by Melvin Morse, a pediatrician. The man who was sitting next to me kept glancing over trying to read the details of my book jacket. He was a pleasant middle aged man dressed in jeans, cowboy boots and a plaid flannel shirt. As I looked up from the pages, he finally said, "Excuse me ma'am, but what are you reading?" I told him it was all about the unusual experiences that children reported to their parents or doctor after they recovered from being close to death. He stared ahead for a moment, then got a puzzled look about his forehead. He looked at me and smiled saying, "You don't believe that do you?" I said "Well, actually I do since I almost died once and had something happen to me that was almost exactly like what these children are saying."

He smiled at me somewhat nervously but his eyes belied his true feeling. He then proceeded to pretend to nap for the next three hours. I went back to my book. I hoped I had not made him too uncomfortable after that exchange. I thought, "Too bad I can't tell him all about it."

DO ALL PEOPLE GO THROUGH THE TUNNEL AND INTO THE LIGHT? WHAT HAPPENS TO BAD PEOPLE?

The overwhelming majority of cases that are reported and thus reflected in published literature are positive experiences...almost of a subjectively heaven-like nature. There are a relatively rare number of cases that have a nightmarish, negative, hellish component. Since this represents a very small number of cases so far, little can be said as to whether these were "bad" people facing judgement and having some type of demonic contact. I would imagine, as difficult as it was for me to convey a very positive experience, this group of experiencers may have an even harder time. Who knows, possibly this group is much larger than we think. Perhaps the few negative reports are just the tip of an iceberg.

I met a woman who had a negative near-death experience. She was in her fifties and nearly died giving birth over thirty years ago. As she began to share her story with me she promptly corrected the use of my word "negative". She said it was not negative . . . just extremely frightening and that she know others who had frightening near-death experiences. As she told me her story I found we had a lot in common. She felt that sense of separation, of movement through a passage but then she experienced fear and torment. She felt as though she was watching a hell-like scene. Inwardly, I shuddered and asked her what she made of that. She pointed out at all times she felt protected and guided through this and it was a powerful lesson for her. She gained insight into how she was to lead her life. She pointed out that she was not a bad person, as I often point out, but took a lot of her life for granted. Finally, she explained it to me this way. It's like a matter of perspective. It's like learning a lesson from two different approaches. Most of her life she felt she learned best from dramatic lessons as these. It was a frightening experience but not negative since it transformed her perspective on life.

ARE NEAR DEATH EXPERIENCES REPORTED FROM OTHER COUNTRIES?

Published articles about the phenomenon of the near death experience are reported from Australia, England, Scotland, China and India. Even in reports from non-western countries, the out-of-body phenomenon, the tunnel experience, meeting the bright light and a life review are common themes.

There are cultural variations in the reports from experiencers of other countries and cultures. For example in a survey conducted in rural China - although over half of those surveyed thought the N.D.E. was a dream or a hallucination - there was knowledge of death bed visions and Buddhists entering the "Pure Land" who had recovered from grave illness.

IS THE NEAR DEATH EXPERIENCE SOMETHING PRETTY NEW? I'VE ONLY HEARD OF IT FROM TIME TO TIME RECENTLY IN POPULAR MAGAZINES.

No, in fact experiences of those who have been seriously ill or injured and near death have been recorded and verbally passed on over many centuries. There have been references to death bed visions for many years. In fact, it is thought that the ancient rituals involving Egypt's pharaohs at the pyramids around 820 A.D. involved near death experiences. The mysterious rites of antiquity involved people being subjected to death (almost) so that they could experience the fact that there really was no death. These survivors are said to have reported experiences upon their recovery that closely compare to the experiences in modern times.

It is possible that there are even greater numbers of people who have had near-death experiences than that which is estimated. Many people now are recovering from illnesses that were previously considered fatal. With the advances in medical technology and widespread use of cardio-pulmonary resuscitation, CPR, survivors exists that would have not before. In spite of the natural reluctance of those to share their experiences due to misunderstanding or ridicule, with the appropriate support, it seems as though more now are going public and people read about it in popular books and magazines.

DOES THE SIMILARITY OF THE N.D.E. (SEPARATION FROM BODY, JOURNEY THROUGH THE TUNNEL, ENTERING THE LIGHT AND A LIFE REVIEW) MEAN EVERYONE GOES TO HEAVEN . . . SAVED OR NOT?

No. The N.D.E. stages, particularly entering the light, represents a journey but only to a certain point. In the light, my life and it's effect on others was revealed with starling truth and clarity. Accountability, integrity, and love was emphasized. I was at a crossroad, however, of some type. We do not know from those who go further what happens then. If the message to me was being held accountable, perhaps I could enter into the unfathomable glory ahead. It makes me concerned, though, to think that also I could go somewhere else or worse yet, remain forever longing and stopped at the "gate" there.

DID YOU SEE GOD?

No. The presence I was entering into was awesome. There are no words to describe the building sense of goodness, love, purity and knowledge that I was experiencing. I knew something so wonderful was ahead and the anticipation was phenomenal. But remember, I was stopped short. My life was shown to me and I returned to my hospital bed knowing I was nearing a source of majestic power but I could not reach it . . . yet.

WERE YOU A CHRISTIAN WHEN YOU HAD YOUR N.D.E?

No. But in 10 months I became one . . . born again. My experience with the light made me aware - not perfect. I had to begin to commit myself and lead my life in accordance with that goodness and purity I experienced in the light. The answer for me became assurance and comfort in a personal relationship with Jesus Christ.

I CAN'T HELP BUT THINK THESE NEAR-DEATH EXPERIENCES ARE A RESULT OF SOME BODILY PROCESS OR PHYSIOLOGICAL CHANGE. WHAT DO THE SCIENTISTS THINK?

A scientific approach to the phenomenon and components of the near-death experience is a very difficult one. Since the experience can only be "observed" indirectly through the reports of the experiencer, this is a challenge. The experience can not be easily defined nor measured. The best method in a general way so far has been to take an orderly approach to the questions asked of the experiencer going from broad, opened-ended questions to the more specific. It has also been very helpful to look at the relationship of the experience to the person having the experience. That is, to relate the N.D.E. to the experiencer's gender, intellect, geographic background, age, religious affiliation, etc. By taking this approach consistently in a variety of studies, a substantial data base has been built so that certain deductions can be made. From this growing data base, questions will be formulated for ongoing scientific research inquiry.

Another approach to the scientific study of the near death experience has been the review of the experiencers' medical records. Documentation of the timing and medical intervention during the experience can help examine relationships between measurable clinical findings and the phenomenon. Examples of quantifiable measurements in the medical record would be the amount and type of medication administered, the level of oxygen in the blood and the brain and the person's vital signs before and after. The medical record would also reveal if indeed the near death expriencer were near death based on the person's clinical condition.

Examination of the experiencer through standardized psychological testing is another way the near death experience can be indirectly measured. Standardized tests with known comparative values, administered to the experiencers, would provide an additional viewpoint from which to observe the experience.

New biological explanations are being proposed by medical scientists who see the strong similarity to these sensations evoked when portions of the central nervous system are stimulated. An association to the stimulation can be seen in persons reporting peripheral clouding (the tunnel) or epileptiform activity (the light). This is an area that admittedly needs a great deal of research as do many other areas. The phenomenon can not be directly observed nor measured by current scientific modalities.

As long as the near death experience continues to have the strong spiritual component, it's essence defies the standard scientific approach. That is, although many studies have looked at the component parts of the near-death experience, the major aspect of the experience that seems to defy science, is its transforming effect on the individual. A lifelong meaningful change of perspective is not the result of a dream, a hallucination or some abnormal discharge of chemicals or electricity in the brain. The secret of the near-death experience calls for an integrated pooling of study involving medicine, the social and psychological sciences and theology. Even then, the true meaning of the near-death experience is a profoundly personal one.

8 MILLION?

The Gallup polls state, that in this country alone, nearly 8 million people report a near-death experience. This number struck me as being quite high. Although I had kept my experience to myself for many years after learning of the responses I would receive, I still found that number hard to believe. It was hard to imagine there are officially reported 8 million experiencers in this country.

Something interesting happened to open my eyes to how many experiencers are truly out there and have had an occurrence like mine.

I was starting to think more frequently about my near death experience. I slowly and cautiously began to share bits and pieces of it with close and trusted friends. My new husband kept asking for more details. I struggled to find the right words to describe what I had gone through. What I was perceiving from him was an openness, possibly a belief, that this experience was not a confabulation created to achieve something else. I struggled to share it with sincerity, honesty and completeness. Finally, after many a straining-for-the-right-words session, I joked with him, "You'll have to read the book." That idea he took matter-of-factly and with enthusiasm. Of course, I went on to write this book. I spoke with others about my experience and found my "story" received mixed reviews. Most people were fascinated, a few others seemed distinctly uncomfortable with the topic. But I found that those who listened, listened very intently and asked many good questions.

I began to ask some questions of myself as well. Although I had significantly changed as a result of my N.D.E., how was this change effecting my practice as a nurse and Trauma Coordinator at a children's hospital? I knew the difference in me but did others? Was there an opportunity to share and support those who cared for children and families of severely ill and injured children? I knew that I now took an open and non-judgmental approach to patients' accounts of "seeing things". I began to wonder was that enough?

I began to undertake this new series of questions as a personal challenge. In my typical pattern of intense curiosity, I decided to study the near death experience. People who know me have often said I think too much. I have always been known as someone who takes things, most things, quite seriously and intently. Every job I ever held, I have always done with intensity and detailed attention. I may not have always had perfect results, but that is the way I go about my life. Back when I was a little girl, I would agonize over the only B+ grade that stood out among the other A's all in a neat row next to every subject. In my job evaluations, I would get all "excellents", but I would always ask my supervisor what he or she thought I could do better. Usually the reply, I got after my supervisor thought awhile, was the recommendation to "lighten up some".

Anyway, I began to tackle this challenge. I learned in graduate school that the first important step to scientific inquiry was to do a complete search of the literature. This way, one would know that information was already available on the subject. That is where I decided to start. My husband and I set up our evening at the downtown library. The research librarian assisted us with a computer search. We found four books in the popular lay literature but could not locate any copies in Fresno or the surrounding area libraries. They were all gone...checked out and long overdue. Undaunted, we requested copies to be sent from the nearest library that had the books available. Now I was excited! Someone had written a book about this. Specifically four people had each written a book about the near death experience. It wasn't until much later that I was to find out how much had been written on the subject. And to think that I considered myself to be well read!

Weeks went by before the first book arrived. I drove downtown on a lunch break to dive into its contents. This book, by Kenneth Ring, was to lead me into a surprisingly rich flow of people and valuable information. I read it in record time. Throughout the book there were numerous names and references. I wrote down every lead. By the time I finished his book I was ready to start studying all I could that was written on the topic. I knew that the author lived in Connecticut. With my persistence I phoned the residence of the author, Dr. Kenneth Ring. He answered the phone. I tripped all over my tongue as I tried to quickly explain myself and what I was trying to do. I still believed that most people upon hearing my story would be quick to end the conversation like the experiences I had with my family. Much to my surprise and relief, he began to tell me about current reputable research papers that were available on the topic. I was also given the name of an organization that had been studying the phenomenon of the near-death experience for many years. There was an organization called the International Association for Near Death Studies (I.A.N.D.S.). Now I had more fascinating reading to do and more interesting people to contact.

Many of the articles I read were cited as having been published in the Journal of Near Death Studies. This journal was still available through I.A.N.D.S.

I read that I.A.N.D.S. was incorporated in 1981, as a non-profit educational and research organization. As a world-wide organization it's members are comprised of scientists, scholars, near-death experiencers and the general public. Their publication impressed me as having a very scientific and established format. It looked at the topic of N.D.E.'s from a variety of perspectives. The contents were written by medical professionals, psychologists, theologians and the eclectic group referred to as "experiencers" . . . those who had a near-death experience.

I found out the name of the current I.A.N.D.S. organization president, Dr. Pat Fenske. Dr. Fenske became invaluable in her encouragement of my studies. I took a trip to her home office in Philadelphia. As I walked into her massive brown row-home of stately classic Philadelphia elegance, I relaxed. I told her about myself. She listened and assured me that there were many others who related experiences of such personally monumental significance. She asked me to call her Pat. She shared a wealth of insight and perspective on the experience as she knew the N.D.E. Our time together was quickly over but she gave me some sample journal copies and additional references to pursue. I photographed her and gave her a hug before I left. I tapped into her strength and committed myself further to my studies. With this armor of excitement and encouragement I was ready to write my story to share with others. I wrote on the plane home. I wrote hours every day for weeks.

I then came across another name in my readings, Dr. Justine Owens. Dr. Owens was a researcher at the University of Virginia. With a credible affiliation like the University of Virginia, I needed to talk with Dr. Owens. I must admit my call to her was not quite as straightforward as it should have been. I introduced myself as a Trauma Coordinator who was doing research in what nurses thought about the N.D.E. I had thought of doing this research but really wanted to know what Dr. Owens was doing and what her research was showing about the N.D.E. After about two minutes of discussion about my study, I "confessed". I told her that I had an experience. You see, as I mentioned before, this type of veiled communication would not have been compatible with my experience with the light. I still assumed that I would be doubted or my call would be politely ended. I was, once again, pleasantly encouraged to describe my experience. I was then asked to consider completing a screening questionnaire to see if I would be an experiencer that their division wished to study further. I agreed. Shortly thereafter I submitted the information and signed a release so that my medical record could be examined as it related to the experience.

Every step of research along the way advanced and confirmed my work. I became more confident in sharing my experience. I could easily compare the detailed similarities and striking differences with the N.D.E.'s of others.

Then I got a phone call back from Dr. Owens. She asked me if I would consider being interviewed as a case example for a feature on N.D.E.'s in *Life* magazine. I was assured of *Life's* professionalism and that the article would be well-done. Considering the reputation and history of *Life* and the encouragement of Dr. Owens, I agreed to be interviewed by writer, Naomi Cutler.

Ms. Cutler asked me a few open ended questions, then I proceeded to tell her about my experience. Although the entire interview was conducted over the phone, it was a very emotional experience. Naomi was an excellent listener and captured the words, the feel and the essence of my N.D.E. She called me to read the story back to me twice. At one reading, her voice cracked. She had become "choked up", overcome with emotion and was moved by the story. All I can say is that she was close to perceiving what the experience was really all about for me.

I had lunch with a co-worker after the story appeared in Life. This nurse recalled a child in our I.C.U. that was referred to the psychologists for repeatedly telling how she went to heaven and saw the angels.

Later my mother-in-law told me when her mother was dying, she saw beautiful colors "up there" above the foot of her bed. Soon I started getting phone calls, unsolicited letters and anonymous cards from people who wanted to share their story with someone they knew would understand. Whenever I spoke to any group of people several would say they also had an experience or they knew of someone or a family member who had. What makes me feel a little sad is that as a nurse over many years, people had tried to tell me about their experiences. I thought I had to do something about it. I thought I had to explain it to families or calm my patients down. Now I know I only had to listen.

AND MORE ACCOUNTS

I received a letter written on a ripped out page of a green steno pad. The return address read that it was from a convalescent hospital in a community north of Fresno. It read: "Dear Doctor: I read with great interest, the article about your experience in the Fresno Bee last Sunday. I, too, had a similar experience during the birth of my first child. Like yourself, it left me much more able to handle and deal with things that have happened in my life during the past almost sixty years. I know death is not the ending, but the beginning!

The woman who wrote the letter, Mary Wilson, offered her story as another "testimony" to add to my book. With that sincere encouragement, I was prompted to call her a few weeks later. I phoned her on her private line at the convalescent hospital. In a voice that was clear yet delicate, she replied that she would be most happy to meet with me and provide more detail about her experience. She had a detectable Southern accent and sounded weak. When I explained that I was not a physician, she laughed and we joked together about how easy that was for me to get an M.D. behind my name. I told her my husband and I would be by after church to visit with her.

The convalescent hospital was a small one-story building with residents strolling slowly beside their nurses and Sunday afternoon visitors. The front entrance door was stuck and a resident inside helped us wrestle the door open. The smell of pine disinfectant hit us as we entered the bright hallway. We were observed with a mixture of expectancy and curiosity. Mary had instructed me to meet her in the living room on the right. We were fifteen minutes early but went into the living room anyway. There was a woman who smiled at our approach, seated in her wheelchair in the far right corner of the room. No one else was in the living room. In the corner was a cornflower-blue parakeet in a silver cage. As we passed by it happily squawked it's greeting at us. Mary explained that the bird does that for all visitors, then she introduced herself as we neared. I liked Mary immediately. When her hand met mine it felt soft and fragile. She smelled of baby powder and laundry detergent. Mary had a warm smile and even through her dark cataract glasses, I could see a twinkling eye. She wore a loose blue and purple print dress and had a baby blue sweater pulled across her shoulders. Her hair was white and simply styled behind her ears.

We sat down near her. She gently folded her hands on her lap and asked how we would like to proceed. Stan and I assured her we had time and that she could take as long as she wanted to tell us her story as she recalled it. She agreed to have me tape record her so I could later listen so as to get all the important details. Mary began her story.

"It happened back in 1934. It was extraordinary. It occurred with the birth of my first child at home after a very long labor. A doctor and his nurse were there and I was in terrible pain. The baby was large and I was having a difficult labor. They had given me medication and I was going in and out of consciousness. They were doing the best they could. Then I had this extraordinary experience. I was suddenly in this vast place, not a tunnel, but a place I had never been in before." Mary struggled for words as she spread her arms out. "I was surrounded and I was nearing this huge light. I was travelling so fast. It was just "whish" and I was there. The light was bright but not too bright. It was shrouded. It was beautiful. I felt so peaceful, it was wonderful, so peaceful...I, I just can't describe it. There were people there. They were happy to see me. I knew who they were. They were my mother and others but I just recognized them somehow, although they had no physical form. I heard them talk to me but not the way you hear people talk. It was as though the ideas went right here," as Mary pointed to her right temple. "I was just fine there and they wanted me to stay. They were so happy, so happy to see me. I told them, in my mind, I couldn't stay. I had to go back to my baby. Then 'whish' ", Mary made a sound indicating her speedy travel, "I was back. I came to. Then I heard the nurse say, 'Oh, no'. My baby was dead. She was a perfect baby girl and they told me the cord entangled during labor so she could not breath."

"After all this, I grieved terribly. I wanted other people's children. I clipped Gerber baby pictures out of magazines. I felt sorry my husband did not take a picture of her. When I thought about what happened to me I thought I must be crazy. When I mentioned it to my husband, he didn't know what to make of it. I went back to my doctor for my six-week check-up and he, well, sort of put it aside, you know. That's how everybody at that time reacted."

"This experience has stayed with me for fifty-eight years now...but there's a lot more. This is important. This is not, well, ridiculous. This all has to do with the way you live life. Religion is here." Mary pointed one of her pink pearly finger nails at the center of her chest. "The peace that came over me was... Well, there is a purpose to the experience. That is to console others. The purpose is to help others. It helped me. After this happened, years later, my daughter died. She was my second child...and I have two more, and grandchildren and great grandchildren. My daughter had spinal surgery. She was a wonderful Christian woman in her forties. She had terrible back pain and died of taking too many prescription medications." Mary's throat tightened as she remembered her daughter's death. "But", she said, "my experience helped me. One night, my departed mother came to me and reminded me that my daughter was in that wonderful, peaceful place. My husband died two years ago. It helped me then. Now I am here, in the convalescent hospital and it is all right. I am not afraid to die. Actually, I am looking forward to that experience again even though I am fine here." Mary explained she had severe osteoarthritis. She had no vision in her left eye and just had cataract surgery on her right. Her life is fulfilled by reading and spending time with visitors. "My children are wonderful", she says. At the hospital though, she says, most of the residents are mentally and physically disabled so she has few friends. Mary was a secretary as she raised her children and felt her experience helped her with the stress of moving from her home in Louisiana forty years ago to California.

Suddenly, Mary looked exhausted. In the background we could hear hymns and clapping coming from another room where a church service was being conducted. Mary asked for a copy of my story and we held hands for a moment. She then placed her small, fragile hands on the wheels of her chair and pivoted herself around and across the room. She needed her rest and we left.

Mary is a magnificent woman with a beautiful story to tell.

* * * *

This is another call I received: "I'm sorry to bother you," the male voice said, "but I just read the newspaper about you. Something like that happened to me. This is not a crank call! In 1977, I was involved in an accident.

I was doing a liquor delivery, a hot shot run, in a vehicle that was not road worthy. Anyway, that doesn't matter. I don't remember the accident itself. After the wreck I was about sixty feet in the air seeing all these people I had never seen before around my body. I felt warm. There was a color but I can't describe it. I could hear a humming sound but couldn't hear anything else. I remember a man hitting me, punching me in the chest. I was upset. I wondered what I had done wrong that he should be hitting me. I was told later in the hospital that my heart had stopped for about four minutes. Since the accident, I was frightened by some really strange things. I was able to know about coming earthquakes. Now I'm used to it. I just send myself dated postmarked letters about the earthquake. Maybe someone will want to study this someday. I have photos of the wreck. The vehicle was demolished."

Fresno, California

* * * *

Another phone call from a woman: "I read your article and I'm sorry to bother you but I want to tell you that this is helping people. I had the same thing happen to me and people thought I was cracked. I was so embarrassed that I didn't tell anyone. Actually, I did tell my children. They were still real little. My kids believed me. This happened to me twenty-four years ago and I'm so glad finally people are starting to talk about it."

* * * *

This was a phone call I got one evening: "I just want to ask you a few questions about your experience. What was it like in the light?" I told him that for me the light was the most pure, wonderful, true, peaceful thing I ever experienced. There is nothing on earth that I can compare it to...it is beyond description. He started interrupting me with excited words of confirmation. He said that he had not told anyone about his experience for years. He didn't even tell his wife since he thought she wouldn't believe him. He told his pastor who just consoled him and his frustration about the N.D.E. He said that he was in an auto accident fifteen years ago. Even to this day, in quite moments he remembers the light. He said that, "The light was...indescribable."

* * * *

I came upon a nurse who worked in the emergency room the day the article came out in the paper. She said, "Grace, I thought you were writing about me". She went on to say that she had a near death experience and for us to get together to have lunch and discuss this further.

* * * *

I got a phone call at work from a nurse who works in the operating room. In 1975, she was hospitalized for severe vaginal bleeding following surgery. She remembers driving herself to the hospital, bleeding all over her car. At the Emergency Room entrance, she remembers a heated argument with the security guard who wouldn't let her park at the entrance...until he saw the blood! She said, "I never made it to the O.R. since the medical staff thought they could control the hemorrhaging with packing done at the bedside." I told the nurse on duty I was bleeding but she told me I wasn't— just as my blood pressure dropped. I was then rushed to the O.R. A resident sat by my bedside all night. I told him what I experienced. He told me that sometimes patients report those types of experiences to him.

* * * *

I received a letter in the mail that was very impressive: The article in yesterday's *Fresno Bee* touched me to the core! I say "Hurrah!" for publicizing your near death experience. "Ye shall know the truth and the truth shall set you free!" I am certain you will be hearing from many people who have read the article in the paper and in *Life*. (I have not found a copy of *Life*). I had a near death experience in 1957, and although it was not as extensive as yours in the sense that I never experienced a cloud of light or a light at the end of the tunnel (as many have), it was for me a wonderful experience that taught me not to fear death. Simply, this is what happened: In April, 1957, I was six months pregnant. On a sunny spring day in Hayward, California, I went for a routine pre-natal checkup with my doctor. While there I asked him to remove some warts from my hands. I had never reacted to novocaine (or any local anesthetic) before so we went ahead with it. When he injected the anesthetic into a wart site on a finger of my right hand it failed to localize and went directly into a vein (or whatever we have in our fingers). I went into a state of shock in under a minute. I had to be laid down because I was fainting. Then I felt myself swell up like a blimp (that feeling), I wanted to kick my shoes off, asked for water (they gave me none). The last "in body" remembrance was me asking for water and the doctor saying no because I would vomit it up. Then I was peacefully floating above the panic stricken doctor and two excited nurses. I felt nothing out of my body. My perception then was very clear, I was comprehending and seeing with a clarity greater than with my human brain or eyes. It was all very interesting to me. I could see the beads of sweat and pallor on the doctor's face. He barked orders to the nurses to get the adrenaline loaded into the syringe. I was totally unconcerned. In that state I wasn't worried about anything but I remember asking myself, "What about the baby?" I immediately answered my own question with "I'll take HER with me." (There was no testing to determine the sex of a baby in those days, before birth. And, the baby was a girl. In my out-of-body state I had that knowledge.) When I was given the "life saving" injection that brought me back it was agony. The adrenaline rush, of course, can be explained, but it was more than that. It was that I really didn't want to come back. I am sure the whole experience didn't last over five minutes. The first thing the doctor said to me when I "awakened" was "My God, you almost died!" He said my blood pressure had plunged to around 20 over some other figure. (I wish I'd written it down). He said he'd never had such an experience before. That was almost 35 years ago. That baby girl was healthy and now lives in Germany. It was not only my experience but hers too, because I could pass on to her the precious legacy that death is nothing to fear. I wish I had experienced the Light you saw but I know when I do leave my physical body behind for good that Light will be there. Thank you for coming out with your story. My story is "small" but you have my permission to share it with anyone who may be interested in it.

E.L.
Fresno, California

* * * *

Your experience and mine give validity to our existence. We are not just a higher form of animal. Someone is watching us.

G. K.
Corpus Christi, Texas

* * * *

I was only twelve and I remember everything that happened. I was swimming in the ocean past the point I was cautioned not to go. A large wave struck me from the side and I was pulled under. I remember struggling and choking but only for a little while. I saw myself from a place outside my body and noticed how it was rolling about below the surface with the waves movements. I felt wonderful as I moved through a dark tunnel toward a warm light. A beautiful man welcomed me and showed me my life like a photo album with all the pages flipping rapidly. I understood so much and didn't want to go but he said, not with words, it wasn't my time. People laugh when I tell them about this so I don't say much about it. I know I'm a better person now. I value my life and I'm not afraid to die.

* * * *

While presenting a talk at the Second Annual Day of Hope for the Compassionate Friends, a support group/ association of bereaved parents, one woman continued to catch my attention. Throughout the entire presentation she clung closely to her teenage daughter. I spoke to her later and she said that her deepest sadness came from the death of her son in a terrible car crash. Other members of the family were injured and she was not there to mother her son at the moment of his death. The message of the near-death experience proved to her that he was now in a far better place and his suffering was only temporary. Her lingering sorrow at her inability to comfort her son was lessened by listening to what it was like when the body stops functioning and another reality begins.

Santa Ana, California

WHEN MY PATIENTS DIE: THEN AND NOW

In the course of my twenty plus year career in nursing, I have seen and cared for many hundreds, perhaps thousands, of people who died. As a result of my personal near death experience, I now look at my patient's dying process differently than I did earlier.

I was able to categorize the deaths of my patients into two very broad groups after watching so many deaths. The two main groups seemed to be people who died in peace and those who died in panic. Another group that actually didn't fit into this classification system occurred. That final group didn't die. Their "time wasn't up." They were my patients that I needed to listen to after their return from their near-death experience.

I'd like to describe two peaceful deaths that immediately come back to my memory after many years. These peaceful deaths were outstanding and they impressed me greatly. As a young nurse, a patient's death always felt like a defeat for me...the ultimate challenge to all the treatment, medications, and specialists that could be summoned to the aid of a critically ill or injured person.

My first encounter with a peaceful death was when I was working as a nurses aide in a nursing home. I was 19 years old at the time and in my second year of undergraduate studies for my nursing degree. I worked weekends and evenings which provided me with added tuition money. Working also gave me an edge over the other students by gaining experience from the extra patient contact. There was one elderly couple in the home that shared a room there. The 90-plus year old gentleman was a retired preacher and his sweet 90-ish wife was the proverbial perfect preacher's wife. They did everything together. They strolled the halls in synchrony. They ate at the same pace. They prayed the same prayers. They had matching snow white hair and had been inseparable since there were teenage sweethearts. Then one day, the Reverend tripped and took a fall in the nursing home hallway. He was put to bed and the next day began to run a fever. He was soon confused, weakened and gave up his spirit and died. His wife knelt by his bed for a day then marched over to her bed and proceeded to run a fever. She was my assigned patient that weekend and I had a sense of foreboding about her. I remained watchful but aside from her fever, there were no impressive signs of severe illness. Yet, I remained worried. They did everything together. To me she looked as though she was going to just go join the Reverend. I leaned over her bed side-rails and watched her eyelids flutter. She had the sweetest smile on her face. She was always smiling anyway. There was a good reason for her perpetual smile. The Mrs. and the Reverend were like a George Burns and Gracie Allen skit. The Reverend would always initiate some dumb joke and the Mrs. would keep the nursing home staff laughing with her incredibly ridiculous punch line. As I watched her I realized she was quietly giggling to herself. I said, "What's so funny?" She held up her hands and rubbed her fingers together. This made no sense so I repeated my question. She opened her twinkling eyes and said to me that the Reverend was "up there" and he asked her how she felt. She was joking back with him that she "felt with her fingers," as she winked at me. She looked up again at the ceiling, or through the ceiling and her respirations stopped.

The other peaceful death patient I remember was an overweight man in his early sixties. I was a staff nurse in an Emergency Department and could see he was very unstable medically as the police officer whisked him into the Code Room. From his appearance, I knew I was working within seconds of his cardiac arrest. The man was breathing slow labored respirations. He was as white as his tee shirt and he was soaked with perspiration. I could feel a thready, irregular pulse in his neck but circulation was already shutting down to his arms and legs. I paged other staff into the room on our intercom. The police officer and I hoisted him up on to the stretcher. I ripped open his shirt and slacks with my scissors and tried to get the monitor wires attached to his soaked chest so that we could keep an accurate eye on his heart's activity. As other staff arrived and fell into their routines, the man grabbed me by my upper arm with a strength that shocked me. He pulled my head close to his lips and gave me instructions quite clearly and coherently. He said, "My son is worried and waiting for me in the waiting room. Go tell him I love him and I'm leaving to be with Jesus." I began a word of protest as he smiled, closed his eyes and the monitor alarm signalled his heart failure. He released his grip on my arm. The code team worked on resuscitating him for almost an hour unsuccessfully. He calmly and quietly passed on.

I said I had two categories. This is an example of the "panic" death. It is quite horrible. These deaths don't necessarily happen in untimely or accidental deaths. I think they occur in people who are not right, not at peace with themselves. These people end their lives in utter turmoil, grasping and panicked in their final hour.

I was a clinical specialist nursing supervisor doing rounds on one of the units with the new oncology unit head nurse. On that floor, patients had various types of cancers in various stages of their diseases. The head nurse stopped me outside of the door of a new admission who had come in over the weekend. It was Monday and this woman had somehow already managed to alienate and/or terrorize the entire 4-East staff. Cigarette smoke leaked out from under her closed hospital room door in her private room. Already we had a few dangerous immediate issues at hand. First, the smoking was unsafe and second, it could burn down the hospital. Now, someone had to go in and administer her chemotherapy and change the pads from her draining wounds. As I cracked open the door, a raspy, shrieking voice loudly commanded that the door be closed. A full water pitcher was hurled across the room at the door. I cajoled my way into the room and faced a woman living in torture. This pitiful woman was only a few years older than I. She had been through three divorces, had several small children who were all in the care of relatives and was battling advanced metasticized uterine cancer. Her family informed me that all her life she had fought with everyone. No one visited her when she went to the hospital any more. She had no one left who cared to be near her. As I stood by her bedside she mocked and belittled me with words so continuously obscene that her sentences made no sense. Since her disease had progressed so far there was little to offer her except pain relief. With trepidation each nurse tried her professional best but each was cast out of the room with the venomous anger. As the days went by, she grew weaker. She would drink none of our F---ing water nor eat any of our F---ing food. She called us all F---ing pigs as she pleaded pitifully for cigarettes. As exhausted as she was though, she would not sleep. We all figured somehow she had to sleep. One day I came in early. It was 5:00 A.M. I observed her in her room from the safety of the doorway. She had propped dinner trays and pillows all around her to keep herself upright. I braved my approach to her bedside. She no longer had the strength to scratch or punch as she used to just a week ago. Now she would only spit on us if we got her angry. I asked her why she was propped up like this. She stared into my very soul and said, "I'm afraid to die and go to hell." Her red eyes were dry from dehydration. If she could have cried, I'm sure she would have. I told the staff to call a priest. She said she was a Catholic at one time. In a half hour the priest arrived. I briefed him in the hallway and we gingerly approached her bedside. She was sitting, propped upright, with open eyes. She was dead.

 I mentioned there was a group that didn't die. Before my near death experience I would have attributed these successful resuscitations to appropriate and timely medical intervention. I believe that appropriate medical intervention assists and supports a person's life. But I have seen equally appropriate medical intervention fail in patients who proceeded to die anyway. What I am saying is that in all of these cases there is something else at work that is determining the patients' physical recovery or lack of it. Medicine can provide the optimal support but at times medical intervention is futile. The problem is knowing or seeing the difference. When a medical team is fully involved in the resuscitation of a patient, it is a very late thought that the patient may be dead. The working assumption is always made that the patient can be brought back to life. This is certainly the way most of us would want to keep the medical team thinking. It becomes increasingly difficult to truly measure the moment of death for a patient when machines can breath for him and keep his blood flowing. When does the spirit, the soul, the real being leave the earthly body? To the person who has had a near death experience, who knows the fact that life continues after death, this is the mystery of it all.

I see my dying patients differently now than I did then. I now realize that they are embarking on to something else. I no longer just see them as having lost their lives but as having begun another life.

PERSONAL TIPS

SUPPORTIVE RESPONSES TO A PERSON RE-
PORTING A NEAR DEATH EXPERIENCE
These are some ideas and suggestions from my
point of view. The integration of my near death experience into my life would have been so much easier if
people took this approach with me. They were full of
doubt and fear about what I said. The positive integration of the experience took me nearly ten years to complete. I still to this day feel I am learning from it. Here
are eight ideas I have that will be a supportive and healthy
approach for those dealing with the need to fully communicate their near-death experience:

1.) LISTEN. Listen with openness and acceptance. You don't need to "buy into" the experience. You
don't need to believe it. The near death experiencer just
desperately needs to share the awesome details of his
journey.

2.)   BE THERE. Be available to the experiencer. Isolation after such a significant occasion is pure torture. The experiencer will need to have access to those who would naturally be there to celebrate or support him on any other significant occasion.

3.)   EXPECT INTENSE FEELINGS TO FOLLOW THE EXPERIENCE. The feelings may be obvious to others or they may be hidden from casual view. Let the experiencer verbalize and work through these feelings.

4.)   CONSIDER PROFESSIONAL THERAPEUTIC SUPPORT. This can aid in the experiencers' ability to put the N.D.E. into perspective as it relates personally.

NON-SUPPORTIVE RESPONSES TO A PERSON REPORTING A NEAR DEATH EXPERIENCE

1.)   DON'T LIE. Near death experiencers are quite alert to all responses when they communicate their experience. Lies are quite transparent when a listener nods his head agreeably while thinking, "This person has lost his mind."

2.)   BE HONEST. The near death experiencer has been through quite an ordeal but is not fragile. Share what you are thinking. "This is hard to believe" is okay to say.

3.) DON'T WHISPER. Near death experiencers have not lost their hearing. Don't tip toe about and share your doubts about the story being told by the experiencer.

4.) DON'T SHUN OR ISOLATE THE EXPERIENCER. You would not leave someone significant to you alone after a birth or a death or even at Christmas. This was a major life event and the near death experiencer needs supportive, accepting friends and family.

MEDICAL STAFF IMPRESSIONS

From my perspective as an experiencer, the vast majority of medical staff have an inadequate understanding of the N.D.E. Rarely does the N.D.E. even get incorporated into the traditional medical education that deals with death and the dying patient. As an "insider" to the various health care professions, I would touch on the topic with doctors, nurses and other members of the health care team. Most typical reactions were scientifically doubtful that the phenomenon really existed. The various descriptions of the N.D.E. components are quickly dismissed as drug reactions, hysteria or a lack of sufficient circulation and oxygen to the brain for example.

I am encouraged, however, to realize that the scientific mind is beginning to open their previously rigid thinking and raise questions and study the near-death experience. There is now a substantial and growing wealth of literature on the topic published in credible journals. Students pursuing higher degrees are selecting this topic as a basis for their master thesis and doctoral dissertation.

I believe there was no way for the scientific community to disregard or minimize an event that is occurring across the country as well as in other cultures and in groups - such as children - thought to be untainted by media reports of the N.D.E.

MEDICAL SCHOOL SURVEY

Members of the medical profession are exposed regularly to the critically ill and injured, therefore, the topic of near death experience has a particular relevance to them. People in our society do not usually die at home anymore, supported by loved ones and a vigilant family doctor. They face their final moments in intensive care units, attached to machines, tubes and other devices. They are surrounded by specialists and subspecialists with an incredible knowledge base of the disease process. But do these specialists know enough about the dying process? What are the physicians taught in medical school? How do they know what to say to a family who reports that their loved one is seeing or experiencing something that can not be seen or assessed by others?

To gain some insight into what is currently taught to medical school students across the country, I structured a telephone survey of forty-nine medical schools. The schools represented 24 states and included both state and private universities.

Each school was approached in this manner:

"We are conducting a research study about patients' experiences with death and dying and would like to ask two brief questions of someone knowledgeable of the medical students curriculum content."

Depending upon the size and complexity of the medical schools that we contacted, our phone question would be passed among various departments until someone could answer the following questions with authority:

QUESTION #1
Is the topic of death and dying
covered with your medical students?
QUESTION #2
Do you teach about the phenomenon
reported by dying patients such as the
near death experience or out-of-body experience?

Of the 49 schools which were surveyed only two refused to answer our questions by phone. The remaining 47 participated in the phone survey. When asked if the topic of death and dying was covered, 44 schools replied yes. Only three schools did not separately cover the topic although it was mentioned with various medical conditions as appropriate. When the schools were asked whether the topic of the near death experience was covered, the response was quite interesting.

A full 30 schools replied yes, that the topic is reviewed with the medical students. It is usually reviewed in special seminars or in the Ethics course. There were 17 schools, however, that did not review the topic of the near death experience with their medical students.

Topic	"yes"	"no"
Death and Dying		
44 replied	(94%)	(6%)
Near Death Experience		
30 replied	(64%)	(36%)

Overall the survey was encouraging. While many medical schools did not teach about the near death experience, the good news is that some now do.

PERSONAL MEANING

Jn the foreward of this book, I shared with you that there were three main lessons that my N.D.E. taught me. My N.D.E. provided me with an incredible clarity of insight, perspective and assurance regarding these revelations.

THERE IS AN AFTERLIFE

The first thing I knew beyond a shadow of a doubt was that I had experienced a glimpse of the eternal. Previous to my N.D.E. I believed in an after-life. Actually, to be completely honest, I hoped for an after-life. My faith in this was such that I had previously considered my own mortality. I believed that upon my death, my "spirit" would go to heaven. I only believed this but always felt a twinge of a doubt. Just suppose that when we die, we're dead and my belief in an after-life was just a way of rejecting the thought that I would turn into so much dust. My N.D.E. changed my belief to what I now call my "knowing". I now know with absolute certainty that what I experienced was what I will experience when I die. This resulted in becoming reborn as a Christian and conducting my life in such a way that the next time I will be able to proceed into that perfect light.

I AM ACCOUNTABLE FOR MY ACTIONS
The second profound insight I had as a direct result of my N.D.E. is that I know I will be held to accountable for how I lead my life. I do not mean that specific good, bad and accomplishments will be under scrutiny, but rather what I faced in my N.D.E. was the reflection upon whether I was true to myself. Of my personal gifts, abilities and circumstances, did I treat my life with value and care? Did I conduct myself in a manner which contributed to the universal good in my everyday activities? In my moments in the light, it was all there for me to see. There was no hiding or justifying myself at that time. I saw myself for what I was and I can only deduce that this was critically important to the eternal journey of my soul.

NO ONE NEED FEAR DYING
Thirdly, I was blessed to experience what I believe was the beginning of my death. I never thought very hard or very long about my own death or what it would feel like. Perhaps I thought it would feel like nothing.

My experience as a nurse watching patients die or assisting their families grieve did not help. Patients seemed to suffer unbearably prior to their death. I also noticed something in many of my patients. They often would look peaceful or relieved or to be experiencing something wonderful just before they clinically died. My N.D.E. taught me that beyond the pain is the most wonderful, blissful experience that can not be fully described in words. Beyond the suffering and pain is really something good.

This does not mean that I am anxious to die...actually quite the opposite. I know now the purpose and meaning of my life while I am here. I know that when I die, there is an incredible eternity of which I just experienced a very small part.

SEEING THE CONNECTIONS

So what was the point? What was the meaning of all this? By some standards, I had abysmally failed at certain areas of my life. Ironically, all of this seemed all right now. I was at peace with myself. I did not need to do anything else except learn from my near-death experience.

What does a "failure" teach a person? After a lifetime of achievement in my career, I had expected to feel successful in this area. My career is not me. It needs to not be me. Somewhere beyond what I do for a living is the living itself. How fortunate people are who know this before it is too late.

In my years of caring for people who are ill or dying, I have seen something that up to now, I never quite understood. When my baby died I had an experience that was left unfinished. Now I understand better. This has to do with living life fully and without regret. There is nothing more tragic than looking into the eyes of a dying person who was not true to himself in his life here on earth. The final hour panic, fear and frantic messages are completely ineffective. I imagined when I saw this in others I was catching a glimpse of hell. People ending their lives which were never really lived is devastating.

Living life is not about happiness and fun. Living life is about living it all. It has to do with feeling the pain and experiencing the joy. It means taking risks and standing out as an individual. It means learning, loving others and trusting in faith. So, again, why is this all okay? I think, for once in my life, I have found peace and a personal reassurance. The anxiety and fear is gone from my personality about dying. Perhaps I felt that I experienced some of the "bad" things people worry about and have come through. Not only have I come through trials, I have grown. Having experienced major losses in life can actually result in a perspective and quality others just cannot know. I fully understand aspects to life and can meaningfully share and support others. There is a contentment to settling into this phase of life. It seems to me that this is an important aspect to reaching the middle of one's life. All the years and experiences preceding were laying the ground work. There is a time, to stop and realize what has been. I have reached a point of satisfaction with no regrets. Now I am stronger and ready to face my future. No longer is the future a black, scary monster of unknowns with death at the end. There will always be unknown but by savoring every moment given to me before, now and to come, I can believe in an inner peace to keep me growing personally and I hope others.

AFTERWORD

Sometimes life seems like a confusion string of events making no sense whatsoever. My life once felt like this. My growing years, my marriage, my career all contained many troubling episodes. These episodes seemed without connection. They each left me with a sense of question. I always wondered why...why did these things happen as they did? Did life just happen to a person? Were people meant to learn or see connections from their experiences?

As years went by I learned. Whether this was a process of time, maturity or spiritual growth doesn't really matter. What matters in life is that there is a connection. Everything in life that I experienced did have specific meaning. Each piece, each experience, every second counted and it still does and always will.

Living life is what it is all about. Living and savoring each moment along the road of life. Integrating it all into a unique personality is life's treasure of value today that God gives each one of us.

STUDY QUESTIONS

I.   DEFINITION OF N.D.E.

    A.   What could account for a partial (separation from the body) versus a complete experience (seeing the "Light", a life review)?

    B.   Could a Near Death Experience only occur when a person is not near death?

    C.   In what ways are N.D.E.'s different from or similar to hallucinations . . . or dreams?

    D.   Why do some people come back to experience nothing rather than a N.D.E.?

    E.   Why would a person have a fearful N.D.E?

II.   TRANSFORMING EFFECTS

    A.   Do you think the transformational effects of a N.D.E. are obvious to friends and family of the experiencers?

    B.   In what ways is the N.D.E. likely to change a persons life? Why?

    C.   What factors would influence a person successfully integrating a N.D.E. into his or her life?

    D.   What would be some of the various reactions of family/friends to a "transformed" experiencer?

III.   CULTURAL, DENOMINATIONAL DIF-
FERENCES
        A.   What would account for a person
claiming to see Jesus versus Buddha versus an angel in
his/her N.D.E?
        B.   Is the N.D.E. consistent with the
teachings of
                Catholicism Jewish
                Buddhism   Agnosticism
                RSI   Atheism
                Christianity
                Why or Why not?

IV.   RELATED PHENOMENON
        A.   What do you think the N.D.E. have
to do with reincarnation?
        B.   Are out of body experiences a part
of a near death experience?
        C.   What is a "Universal Conscious-
ness"?
        D.   Does the N.D.E. have implications
regarding:
                1.)   Suicide
                2.)   Abortion
                3.)   Evolution

V.   REAL LIFE APPLICATION

A.   What would be an appropriate response to a friend that just told you he thinks he had a near death experience?

B.   Does the N.D.E. carry any specific message to the bereaved?

C.   What can health care providers and caretakers use from the N.D.E?

D.   How does the N.D.E. apply specifically to my life?

RECOMMENDED READING ON NEAR DEATH EXPERIENCES

1.   Becker, CB Ph.D.: Extrasensory Perception, Near-Death Experiences, and the Limits of Scientific Knowledge, J of Near-Death Studies, 9(1):Fall 1990

2.   Blackmore, S and Troscianko, T: The Physiology of the Tunnel, J of Near-Death Studies 8(1):Fall 1989

3.   Callanan, Maggie and Kelley, Patricia. Final Gifts. New York: Poseidon Press, 1992.

4.   Dougherty, CM MN RN: The Near-Death Experience as a Major Life Transition, Holistic News 4(3): 1990

5.   Gibbs, JC: Three Perspectives on Tragedy and Suffering, the Relevance of Near-Death Experience Research, J of Psychology and Theology 16(1): 1988

6.   Greyson, B MD: Editorial Can Science Explain the Near-Death Experience? J of Near-Death Studies 8(2):Winter 1989

7.   Habermas, Gary and Moreland, J.P. Immortality, The Other Side of Death, Nelson Publishers, Nashville, 1992.

8. Hayes, E and Waters, L: Interdisciplinary Perceptions of the Near-Death Experience Implications for Professional Education and Practice, Death Studies 13:443-453:1989

9. Holden, J Ed.D. and Joesten, L: Near-Death Veridicality Research in the Hospital Setting Problems and Promise, J of Near-Death Studies 9(1):Fall 1990

10. Holden, JM Ed.D.: Unexpected Findings in a Study of Visual Perception During the Naturalistic Near-Death Out-of-Body Experience, J of Near-Death Studies 7(3):Spring 1989

11. Holden, JM Ed,D.: Visual Perception During Naturalistic Near-Death Out-of-Body Experience, J of Near-Death Studies 7(2):Winter 1988

12. Irwin, H Ph.D.: The Devil in Heaven A Near Death Experience With Both Positive and Negative Facets, J of Near-Death Studies, 7(1):Fall 1988

13. Irwin H: Images of Heaven, Parapsychology Review 18(1):Jan-Feb 1987

14. Kellehear, A Ph.D. and Heaven, P Ph.D.: Community Attitudes Toward Near-Death Experiences An Australian Study, J of Near-Death Studies 7(3):Spring 1989

15.   Kubler-Ross, Elizabeth, On Death and Dying, Collier Books, New York, 1969

16.   Kubler-Ross, Elizabeth, On Life After Death, Celestial Arts, Berkeley, CA 1991

17.   Levine, Stephen. Who Dies? An Investigation of Conscious Living and Conscious Dying. New York: Achor Press, 1982.

18.   Milstein, J M.D. and Morse, M M.D. and Venecia D. Jr. M.D.: Near-Death Experiences a Neurophysiologic Explanatory Model, J of Near-Death Studies 8(1):Fall 1989

19.   Moody, Raymond A., The Light Beyond, Bantam Books, New York, 1989

20.   Moody, Raymond A., Life After Life, Bantam Books, New York, 1975
21.   Moody, Raymond A., Reflections On Life After Life, Bantam Books, New York, 1977

22.   Morse, Melvin, Closer to the Light, Ivy Books, New York, 1990

23.   Morse, Melvin, Transformed by the Light, Villard Books, New York, 1992

24. Ego, Moral, and Faith Development in Near-Death Experiencers Three Case Studies, J of Near-Death Studies 7(2):Winter 1988

25. Osis, Karlis, and Haraldsson, Erlendur. At the Hour of Death. New York: Hastings House Publishers, 1986.

26. Owens, J.E. and Cook, E.W. and Stevenson, I.: Features of Near-Death Experience in Relation to Whether or not Patients were Near Death, Lancet Vol 336:Novc 1990

27. Punzak, D: The Use of Near-Death Phenomena in Theraphy, J of Near-Death Studies, 78(3):Spring 1989

28. Rawlings, Maurice, Beyond Death's Door, Bantam Books, New York, 1978

29. Ring, K: From Alpha to Omega Ancient Mysteries and the Near-Death Experience, J of Near-Death Studies 5(2)

30. Ring, K: Heading Toward Omega, William Morrow & Co., Inc., NY 1984

31. Saavedra-Aguilar, J M.D. and Gomez-Jeria, JS Lic.Q.: A Neurobiological Model for Near-

Death Experiences, J of Near-Death Studies 7(4):Summer 1989

32.   Serdahely, W Ph.D.: A Pediatric Near-Death Experience Tunnel Variants, Omega 20(1):1989-90

33.   Serdahely, W Ph.D. and Walker, B: A Near-Death Experience at Birth, Death Studies 14:1990

34.   Serdahely, W Ph.D.: The Near-Death Experience is the Presence Always The Higher Self? Omega 18(2):1987-88

35.   Serdahely, W Ph.D.: Pediatric Near-Death Experiences, J of Near-Death Studies 9(1):Fall 1990

36.   Persons Reporting Near-Death Experiences Really Near Death A Study of Medical Records, Omega 20(1):1989-90

37.   Sutherland, C B.A.: Changes in Religious Beliefs, Attitudes, and Practices Following Near-Death Experiences An Australian Study, J of Near-Death Studies 9(1):Fall 1990

38.   Sutherland, C. B.A.: Psychic Phenomena Following Near-Death Experiences An Australian Study, J of Near-Death Studies 8(2):Winter 1989

113

39. Thornburg, N: <u>Development of the Near-Death Phenomena Knowledge and Attitudes Questionnaire</u>, J of Near-Death Studies, 6(4):Summer 1988

40. Walker, B: <u>Health Care Professionals and the Near-Death Experience</u>, Death Studies 13:1989

41. Wren-Lewis, J: <u>The Darkness of God A Personal Report on Consciousness Transformation Through an Encounter with Death</u>, J of Humanistic Psychology 28(2):Spring 1988

For additional information either about other
books, tapes, or speaking engagements

Call

1-800-545-0076

or

(209) 431-0381
(209) 435-3743 (FAX)
2350 W. Shaw, Suite 103
Fresno, California 93711

If this book is unavailable in local bookstores,
additional copies may be purchased by writing to the
above address.